THE PATH TO SUCCESS

Unlocking God's Blessings

Dr. Lucious Cooper, Jr.

Copyright © 2025 by Lucious Cooper.

All rights reserved. No part of this book may be used or reproduced in any form whatsoever without written permission except in the case of brief quotations in critical articles or reviews.

Printed in the United States of America.

For more information, or to book an event, contact :

(luciouscooper@gmail.com & Website)

http://www.website.com

Book design by KDP Digital Publishers

Cover design by Name of Designer)

ISBN - Paperback: 978-1-967623-40-2

ISBN - Hardcover : 978-1-967623-41-9

ISBN - eBook : 978-1-967623-42-6

First Edition: February 2025

DEDICATION

This book is dedicated to all those who seek a life of purpose and fulfillment, guided by faith and the unwavering love of God. To those who strive for success not merely as a worldly achievement, but as a journey of spiritual growth and positive impact on the lives of others. It is dedicated to the countless individuals who have demonstrated the power of faith in overcoming obstacles and achieving remarkable things, proving that true success is measured not solely by material wealth, but by the richness of a life lived in accordance with God's plan.

May these pages serve as a beacon of hope and inspiration, reminding you of the boundless possibilities that unfold when faith and determination intertwine. This is for those who are courageous enough to embark on this transformative journey, knowing that with God's guidance, even the most challenging paths lead to a destination far exceeding earthly expectations. It is a testament to the transformative power of faith, perseverance, and the enduring grace of our Heavenly Father. May it inspire you to reach for your highest potential and to live a life that honors God and blesses others.

To every seeker, every striver, every believer, this book is dedicated to you. May it ignite within you a renewed sense of hope, purpose, and faith in the journey ahead. May it be a constant reminder that true and lasting success is found not in material possessions or worldly acclaim, but in a life fully surrendered to God's loving purpose.

Table of contens

Preface

Introduction 1

Chapter 1: Defining success through a biblical lens 3

Chapter 2: God's promises and their relevance to success ... 7

Chapter 3: Humility the cornerstone of biblical success 11

Chapter 4: Faith the driving force behind achievement 16

Chapter 5: Trust in god's providence 20

Chapter 6: Diligence and perseverance keys to success ... 25

Chapter 7: Wisdom and discernment in decision making .. 30

Chapter 8: Integrity building trust and reputation 34

Chapter 9: Handling challenges and setbacks with faith ... 39

Chapter 10: Gratitude recognizing gods' blessings 44

Chapter 11: The importance of strong relationships 49

Chapter 12: Generosity and giving back to others 54

Chapter 13: Mentorship and discipleship guiding others 59

Chapter 14: Leaving a positive legacy for future generations ... 64

Chapter 15: Living a life that honors god 68

Chapter 16: Applying biblical wisdom to finances 73

Chapter 17: Integrating faith in career and work 78

Chapter 18: Building strong family relationships 83

Chapter 19: Overcoming temptation and maintaining integrity ... 88

Chapter 20: Developiing a growth mind set   93

Chapter 21: The power of prayer and meditation   98

Chapter 22: Bible study and spiritual growth   104

Chapter 23: Fasting and spiritual renewal   109

Author biography   114

PREFACE

The pursuit of success is a universal aspiration, yet its definition often remains elusive. Many chase after wealth, fame, and power, only to find themselves empty and unfulfilled. This book proposes a different perspective, rooted firmly in the wisdom and guidance found within the Holy Scriptures. It is a journey, not a destination; a path illuminated by faith, guided by God's blessings, and paved with the principles of humility, perseverance, and unwavering trust.

Throughout these chapters, we will explore the biblical foundations of success, delving into the lives of biblical figures to reveal timeless truths applicable to modern life. We will examine key character traits – humility, diligence, wisdom, integrity – that form the bedrock of a life well-lived and a journey toward lasting fulfillment. This is not a simplistic prosperity gospel approach; rather, it is a balanced perspective that acknowledges both the spiritual and material aspects of a life blessed by God.

We will address how faith is not merely a belief system, but an active force that empowers us to overcome challenges, persevere through adversity, and ultimately achieve our goals in alignment with God's plan. This book is designed to be more than just a read; it's a guide, a companion, and a source of encouragement on your individual path. It invites introspection, application, and a conscious integration of faith into every aspect of your life's pursuits. Remember that true success is a tapestry woven from spiritual growth, meaningful relationships, and a legacy built upon the foundation of God's grace. May this journey illuminate the path towards a life of abundance – an abundance not just of material blessings, but of purpose, joy, and lasting peace.

INTRODUCTION

In a world that often equates success with material wealth and worldly achievements, this book offers a refreshing perspective grounded in the timeless wisdom of the Bible. It's a journey into understanding success not as a destination, but as a process – a dynamic interplay between faith, hard work, and God's grace. We will delve into the scriptures, examining the lives of biblical figures who faced extraordinary challenges and demonstrated remarkable faith. Joseph's perseverance, David's trust in God, Esther's courage– these examples, and many others, serve as powerful illustrations of how faith can fuel our endeavors and guide us toward achieving our God-given potential.

This book is not about getting rich quickly or achieving instant gratification; rather, it's about cultivating the character traits that lead to lasting fulfillment and a positive impact on the world. We will explore the importance of humility, diligence, wisdom, integrity, and gratitude – virtues that, when rooted in faith, become powerful tools for overcoming obstacles and achieving lasting success.

This book will equip you with practical strategies and biblical insights to navigate the challenges of life while maintaining a steadfast faith. It will encourage you to integrate your spiritual beliefs into your daily life, making your faith not just a Sunday morning activity, but the foundation upon which you build your dreams.

This work seeks to inspire you, challenge you, and empower you to create a life that honors God and blesses others. It's an invitation to embark on a transformative journey, guided by the scriptures and propelled by the unwavering belief that with God, all things are possible. Remember, true success transcends material possessions; it is found in the richness of a life lived in accordance with God's will, characterized by spiritual growth and a lasting positive impact on the lives of others. This book is your companion on that journey.

CHAPTER 1

DEFINING SUCCESS THROUGH A BIBLICAL LENS

Defining success is a multifaceted endeavor, often shaped by societal norms and personal aspirations. However, this book proposes a paradigm shift: defining success through a Biblical lens. This approach transcends the materialistic measures often emphasized in secular culture, focusing instead on a holistic understanding of well-being that encompasses spiritual growth, positive impact on others, and alignment with God's purpose. This is not to diminish the importance of material provision; rather, it's about placing it within the broader context of a life lived in accordance with divine principles.

The Bible offers a rich tapestry of narratives and teachings that illuminate the nature of true success. It's not solely about accumulating wealth or achieving worldly recognition, although these things may be byproducts of a life lived righteously. Instead, Scripture emphasizes the importance of a deep and abiding relationship with God as the foundation upon which genuine success is built. Proverbs 3:5-6 encapsulates this beautifully: "Trust in the Lord with all your heart and lean not on your own understanding; in all your ways submit to him, and he will make your paths straight." This verse points to the crucial role of faith, trust, and submission to God's will as the cornerstones of a successful life.

Consider the life of Joseph, a pivotal figure in the Old Testament. He experienced immense hardship, betrayal, and imprisonment, yet his unwavering faith and obedience to God ultimately led him to a position of immense power and influence in Egypt. His story demonstrates that success, as defined biblically, isn't always a linear progression devoid of obstacles. Instead, it's often forged through trials and tribulations that refine character and deepen faith. Joseph's ability to forgive his brothers, despite their heinous actions, showcases the transformative power of grace and mercy, traits that contribute significantly to a spiritually rich and fulfilling life. His eventual elevation highlights the often-unforeseen blessings that accompany a life lived in accordance with God's plan. The success wasn't merely about his position, but his integrity, his faithfulness, and his ultimately positive impact on countless lives.

Similarly, the life of Esther, a Jewish woman who became queen of Persia, exemplifies the potential for significant positive influence. Faced with the threat of genocide against her people, Esther bravely risked her own life to intercede with the king. Her courage and faith in God led to the salvation of her entire nation. Esther's story highlights the profound impact a single individual can have when guided by faith and a commitment to righteous action. Her success isn't measured by material possessions or earthly power, but by the lives she saved and the legacy of courage and faith she left behind. Her story resonates powerfully with the biblical definition of success, emphasizing the importance of using one's gifts and position for the betterment of others.

Conversely, consider the examples of those who sought success solely through worldly means, neglecting their spiritual lives. Their stories often serve as cautionary tales, revealing the emptiness and ultimately unsatisfying nature of a life devoid of a genuine relationship with God. The

Bible frequently warns against the allure of riches and power without corresponding spiritual growth, highlighting the dangers of pride, greed, and the pursuit of material wealth at the expense of ethical behavior.

It's important to distinguish the approach presented in this book from the "prosperity gospel," a theology that often links faith directly to material wealth. While the Bible does acknowledge God's provision and blessings, the prosperity gospel's emphasis on material wealth as a primary indicator of God's favor is a misinterpretation. This book takes a balanced perspective, acknowledging both the possibility of material blessings and the far greater importance of spiritual growth, inner peace, and a positive impact on the world as central elements of true success. The focus is on living a life pleasing to God, trusting in His providence, and being content with His provision, regardless of material possessions. While financial security is a legitimate goal, it shouldn't be the sole measure of success.

The Bible teaches that genuine success comes from aligning one's life with God's will, seeking His guidance in all aspects of life, and using one's talents and abilities to serve others. This involves cultivating virtues like humility, integrity, diligence, perseverance, and compassion. It involves facing challenges with faith, trusting in God's timing, and celebrating both big and small victories along the way. It's about building meaningful relationships, nurturing one's family, and leaving a positive legacy for future generations.

The Psalmist, in Psalm 1:1-3, beautifully illustrates this holistic definition of success: "Blessed is the one who does not walk in step with the wicked or stand in the way that sinners take or sit in the company of mockers, but whose delight is in the law of the Lord, and who meditates on his law day and night. That person is like a tree planted by streams of water, which yields its fruit in season and whose leaf does not wither—whatever they do prospers." Here, success is portrayed not merely as material prosperity, but as a life deeply rooted in God's word, bearing fruit in season, and enduring through life's storms. This is the essence of a life truly blessed and successful according to a Biblical worldview. It's a life marked not by fleeting worldly achievements but by a deep and abiding relationship with God, a commitment to righteousness, and a positive influence on the world around us. The following chapters will delve deeper into these principles, exploring specific biblical examples, offering practical advice, and providing strategies for integrating faith into every aspect of your life. The journey toward biblical success is not a race, but a continuous process of growth, learning, and reliance on God's grace. It is a journey of faith, perseverance, and unwavering trust in the One who holds the ultimate plan for your life. This is a journey that promises fulfillment far beyond the fleeting satisfaction of worldly achievements. It's a path that leads to a life of purpose, peace, and lasting significance – a life truly successful in God's eyes.

CHAPTER 2

GOD'S PROMISES AND THEIR RELEVANCE TO SUCCESS

The foundation of a life lived successfully, as defined by biblical principles, rests not only on understanding God's character and will but also on embracing the unwavering promises He has made to His people. These promises, scattered throughout scripture, act as beacons of hope, pillars of strength, and anchors of faith during life's inevitable storms. They are not empty pronouncements but active assurances, offering comfort, guidance, and the promise of divine intervention. Understanding and believing in these promises are crucial in building resilience, fostering confidence, and navigating the complexities of achieving success in a manner that aligns with God's purposes.

One of the most prevalent themes in scripture is God's promise of provision. Psalm 23:1 assures us, "The Lord is my shepherd, I lack nothing." This isn't a guarantee of material wealth, but a declaration of God's sufficiency. It speaks to a deeper truth: that our needs, both physical and spiritual, are met by a loving and compassionate God. This understanding combats the anxieties associated with pursuing success. When we trust in God's provision, we're freed from the relentless pressure to achieve solely for material gain, allowing us to focus on the pursuit of excellence fueled by faith and purpose. This doesn't imply passive reliance; rather, it's an active trust that allows us to work diligently, knowing that our efforts are blessed and supported by a higher power. We can find countless examples in scripture where individuals experienced periods of scarcity yet remained faithful, trusting in God's promise of sustenance. The widow in 1 Kings 17, for instance, faced imminent starvation yet relied on God's promise, ultimately finding her jar of flour and oil miraculously replenished.

Beyond material provision, God promises guidance and direction. Proverbs 3:5-6, previously mentioned, highlights the importance of trusting in the Lord and submitting to His will. This is not a passive resignation to fate but an active seeking of God's wisdom and direction through prayer, scripture study, and seeking counsel from trusted spiritual mentors. When we humbly submit to God's plan, we open ourselves to His guidance, avoiding pitfalls and navigating challenges with greater clarity. This guidance isn't always a direct, audible voice, but it often comes through intuition, circumstances, and the counsel of others who are walking in alignment with God's will. The Israelites, repeatedly straying from God's path, faced countless hardships, highlighting the importance of seeking and heeding His guidance. Conversely, moments of clarity and success often arrived when they humbly returned to His word and sought His direction.

Furthermore, God promises protection and strength during times of adversity. Psalm 91:1-2 declares, "Whoever dwells in the shelter of the Most High will rest in the shadow of the Almighty. I will say of the Lord, "He is my refuge and my fortress, my God, in whom I trust." This promise isn't about avoiding all hardship, but about-facing trials with the confidence that God is with us, offering strength and comfort in the midst of the storm. This protection isn't always a physical shield against harm, but a spiritual fortification that sustains us through challenges. The story of Daniel, thrown into the lion's den, exemplifies this protection, showcasing God's supernatural intervention in safeguarding those who remain faithful. His faith and trust in God's protection wasn't naïve; it was a deep conviction that sustained him and ultimately resulted in his deliverance.

It's crucial to understand that God's promises are conditional on our faithfulness and obedience. While He promises provision, guidance, and protection, He also calls us to act in accordance with His will. This involves cultivating virtues such as humility, integrity, diligence, and perseverance. The promises are not a license for laziness or passivity but rather an empowerment to strive for excellence with a trust that surpasses human understanding. Consider the parable of the talents (Matthew 25:14-30). Those who diligently used the talents entrusted to them were rewarded, not because they were inherently more capable, but because they acted in accordance with God's will, utilizing the resources He had provided. Their success wasn't merely a product of their innate abilities but a result of their faithfulness and diligent efforts.

The timing of God's blessings is often different from our own expectations. This is where unwavering faith and trust in divine timing become critical. We may strive for success, yet the timing of its manifestation might not align with our personal timelines. This doesn't negate God's promises but requires patience, perseverance, and a commitment to staying the course, even when the path seems arduous and the results are delayed. Joseph's story is a powerful illustration of this. Years of unjust imprisonment preceded his rise to power. His unwavering faith in God's plan, even during protracted periods of hardship, ultimately led to a position of immense influence and positive impact. His patience and trust in God's timing highlight the importance of perseverance in the face of delayed gratification. Moreover, acceptance ofing God's plan, even when it doesn't conform to our desires, is crucial in embracing true success according to biblical principles.

This doesn't imply passive acceptance of suffering, but rather an understanding that God's ways are higher than our ways (Isaiah 55:9). Sometimes, the paths He leads us down are challenging and may not seem to align with what we perceive as success. Yet, through these trials, we grow in faith, resilience, and character. The refining process often leads to unforeseen opportunities and blessings that surpass our initial expectations. It's in the acceptance of God's will that we find true peace and a deeper understanding of His purpose for our lives.

God's promises, therefore, are not merely comforting words but dynamic assurances designed to guide us toward a life of purpose, impact, and enduring fulfilment. They provide the foundation upon which a life of biblical success is built, offering strength in adversity, guidance in uncertainty, and the assurance of divine provision. It's through faith in these promises, coupled with diligent effort and unwavering obedience, that we can achieve a level of success that transcends material gain, focusing instead on spiritual growth, positive impact, and a legacy that honors God. Embracing God's promises isn't a passive endeavour; it's an active choice to trust in His plan, even when life's complexities challenge our understanding. It's a journey of faith, patience, and persistent reliance on the power and unwavering love of our Creator.

CHAPTER 3

HUMILITY THE CORNERSTONE OF BIBLICAL SUCCESS

Humility, often overlooked in the pursuit of worldly success, stands as a cornerstone of biblical achievement. It's not merely a pleasant character trait but a fundamental principle that unlocks God's blessings and facilitates genuine, lasting success. Scripture repeatedly emphasizes the dangers of pride and the rewards of humility, painting a vivid picture of how this virtue aligns perfectly with God's plan for our lives. The pursuit of success, when devoid of humility, often becomes a self-serving ambition, leading to spiritual stagnation and, ultimately, emptiness. Conversely, a humble approach, marked by a recognition of God's sovereignty and a willingness to serve others, paves the way for remarkable achievements that extend far beyond material wealth.

Consider the life of Moses, a man chosen by God to lead the Israelites out of slavery. Moses, despite his undeniable leadership capabilities and direct communication with God, consistently demonstrated remarkable humility. He repeatedly questioned his own suitability for the task, expressing his inadequacy before the Almighty (Exodus 3:11, 4:10-13). This wasn't a display of weakness but a profound recognition of God's power and a deep understanding of his own limitations. Moses' humility allowed God to work through him, accomplishing what would have been impossible through a prideful leader. His meekness facilitated God's power, demonstrating that genuine greatness stems not from self-promotion but from selfless service guided by faith.

Similarly, King David, despite his anointing as king and numerous military victories, maintained a posture of humility before God. He frequently acknowledged his reliance on God's guidance and protection, attributing his triumphs to divine intervention (Psalm 28:7, 1 Samuel 17).

David's humility wasn't about self-deprecation; it was an authentic acknowledgement of God's sovereignty. He understood that his achievements weren't due to his own abilities alone but were the result of God's grace and favor. This deep-seated humility shaped his reign, contributing to his overall success as a leader and his enduring legacy as a man after God's own heart. His psalms often express this profound humility and his reliance on God, creating a powerful legacy that resonates even today. David's life serves as a potent example of how humility can coexist with significant achievement, even in positions of great power and influence.

The antithesis of humility – pride, and arrogance – are consistently portrayed in scripture as detrimental to spiritual and personal success. The story of King Nebuchadnezzar, a powerful Babylonian king, serves as a cautionary tale. Nebuchadnezzar's pride and arrogance led him to believe that his own power and accomplishments were the source of his success (Daniel 4). His inflated ego blinded him to his dependence on God, ultimately resulting in a humbling experience that stripped him of his power and sanity. His eventual return to humility, after acknowledging God's sovereignty, marked a turning point, demonstrating the transformative power of acknowledging one's limitations.

Nebuchadnezzar's story is a stark reminder that pride can lead to a precipitous fall, while humility sets the stage for a life transformed by God's grace.

The parable of the talents (Matthew 25:14-30) further illustrates the importance of humility in success. The servant who buried his talent, fearing failure, was not necessarily inherently lazy or incompetent. However, his lack of initiative and his fear of failure stemmed from a lack of humility. He lacked the courage to take risks, to trust God with the potential outcome, and to embrace the opportunities that were presented to him. This underscores that humility isn't about passively accepting one's fate; it's about courageously embracing opportunities, while acknowledging that success is not solely dependent on our own efforts. It's a recognition that our talents are gifts from God, to be used for His glory and the benefit of others.

Cultivating humility isn't a passive endeavor; it requires conscious and consistent effort. Firstly, we must strive for a realistic self-assessment. This involves acknowledging our strengths and weaknesses honestly, without exaggerating either. It requires recognizing our limitations and seeking guidance from others. Prayerful reflection and introspection play a vital role in this process. Seeking feedback from trusted mentors and friends can also provide valuable perspectives that help us gain a clearer understanding of ourselves.

Secondly, we must actively practice gratitude. A grateful heart is a humble heart. When we focus on the blessings in our lives, both big and small, we are less likely to succumb to pride. Regularly expressing gratitude to God, for His provision, guidance, and protection, cultivates a spirit of humility and dependence on Him. Maintaining a gratitude journal or simply taking time each day to reflect on our blessings can significantly influence our perspective and cultivate a more humble attitude.

Thirdly, we should actively seek opportunities for service. Serving others helps us shift our focus from ourselves to the needs of others. It reminds us that we are part of a larger community and that our talents and abilities are not meant to be hoarded but to be used for the benefit of others. Volunteering time, offering assistance to those in need, or simply performing acts of kindness towards others are tangible ways to cultivate humility and to break down self-centeredness.

Fourthly, we must learn from our mistakes. Humility involves admitting when we are wrong, learning from our failures, and seeking forgiveness. It's about being willing to acknowledge our shortcomings, rather than trying to conceal or deny them. A willingness to admit fault, coupled with a genuine desire for improvement, demonstrates humility and sets the stage for personal growth.

Finally, and perhaps most importantly, we must constantly remember that all our accomplishments are ultimately gifts from God. Our talents, abilities, and opportunities are not solely the product of our own efforts but are blessings bestowed upon us by a loving and gracious God. Acknowledging God's role in our success prevents us from becoming self-congratulatory and fosters a spirit of humility and gratitude. It allows us to give credit where credit is due, ultimately acknowledging the source of all good things.

In conclusion, humility is not an obstacle to success but a catalyst for it. By embracing humility, we align ourselves with God's plan, allowing His power to work through us in ways that exceed our own capabilities. It enables us to receive His blessings, navigate challenges with grace, and build relationships that are characterized by mutual respect and understanding. The pursuit of success, therefore, should be undertaken with a spirit of humility, acknowledging our dependence on God, and striving to serve others as a reflection of His love. This approach leads not only to worldly achievements but also to a deeper sense of purpose, fulfillment, and a legacy that honors God. The path to biblical success, therefore, isn't paved with arrogance and self-promotion, but with humility, gratitude, and selfless service—a journey that leads to a life of enduring significance and lasting impact.

CHAPTER 4

FAITH THE DRIVING FORCE BEHIND ACHIEVEMENT

Faith, the unwavering belief in God and His promises, transcends mere optimism; it becomes the bedrock upon which remarkable achievements are built. It's not a passive acceptance of destiny, but an active partnership with the divine, a collaborative effort where God's power and our efforts intertwine to achieve His purposes. This is not about blind faith, but a faith informed by Scripture, prayer, and a deep understanding of God's character and His promises. It is the unwavering conviction that God is able to do immeasurably more than all we ask or imagine (Ephesians 3:20), a conviction that fuels perseverance through adversity and empowers us to pursue goals aligned with His will.

The Bible is replete with examples of individuals whose unwavering faith propelled them to extraordinary accomplishments. Consider Abraham, the father of faith. Called by God to leave his homeland and journey to an unknown land, Abraham's obedience stemmed from an unshakeable faith in God's promises. He believed God's word, even when it seemed impossible – the promise of a vast posterity from a barren wife, the inheritance of a land he had yet to see, and the covenant established through circumcision. His faith was tested repeatedly, yet his unwavering trust in God's faithfulness remains a testament to the power of belief (Genesis 12-15). Abraham's journey, though filled with hardship, showcases that faith isn't blind acceptance, but a confident trust, even amidst uncertainty. Similarly, Joseph, sold into slavery by his brothers, endured years of hardship and false accusations. Yet, his unwavering faith in God's plan never faltered. He remained faithful to God's moral standards even when facing immense temptation and adversity. His eventual elevation to second-in-command in Egypt, a position that allowed him to save his family from famine, underscores the transformative power of faith in the face of seemingly insurmountable obstacles (Genesis 37-50). Joseph's story highlights the significance of maintaining integrity, even under pressure. His steadfast faith allowed him to find purpose in suffering, transforming a devastating circumstance into a tool of divine purpose.

The Israelites' journey through the wilderness, though marked by doubt and rebellion, provides another compelling example. Their escape from slavery in Egypt, guided by Moses' unwavering faith and God's miraculous intervention, was predicated on their belief in God's power. The parting of the Red Sea, the provision of manna, and the guidance by a pillar of cloud and fire all serve as vivid reminders of God's faithfulness and the power of a community united in faith (Exodus 14-18, 16). However, the Israelites often wavered in their faith, succumbing to fear and doubt, showing the importance of consistently nurturing and strengthening one's faith. Their journey underscores the continuous need for faith, even after experiencing miraculous signs.

Faith, however, is not merely a passive belief; it's an active engagement with God. It involves consistent prayer, seeking God's guidance in decision-making, and actively listening for His direction. Prayer is not simply a request list, but a communion with God, a conversation where we pour out our hearts, seek wisdom, and receive strength. It's through prayer that we align our goals with His will, gaining clarity and direction on our paths. Seeking God's will isn't about finding a mystical roadmap to success, but about aligning our aspirations with His purposes, and understanding that true success is measured not merely by worldly achievements but by our spiritual growth and our contribution to His kingdom.

The process of seeking God's will often involves seeking counsel from trusted spiritual mentors, studying Scripture, and reflecting on His past actions in our lives. It's a journey of discerning His voice amidst the noise of the world, a journey that requires patience, humility, and a willingness to submit to His guidance. This active pursuit of God's direction ensures that our achievements are aligned with His purpose, leading to a life of purpose and fulfillment.

Strengthening faith, particularly during challenging times, requires conscious effort and intentional practices. Regular Bible study helps us understand God's character, His promises, and His faithfulness throughout history. Surrounding ourselves with a supportive faith community can provide encouragement, accountability, and a shared experience of God's presence. Journaling our spiritual journey, recording our prayers, and reflecting on God's provision in our lives helps strengthen our faith by reminding us of His consistent presence and faithfulness. Serving others and demonstrating acts of love towards our neighbors is an external manifestation of our internal faith, deepening our relationship with God. It's through actively living out our faith that we reinforce its strength, transforming our beliefs into tangible actions.

It's crucial to differentiate genuine faith from mere wishful thinking. Wishful thinking is a passive hope, based on personal desires and lacking a foundation of trust in God's promises. It's a hope that withers in the face of adversity. Faith, on the other hand, is an unwavering belief in God's power and promises, despite the presence of doubts and challenges.

It's a confident expectation, rooted in a deep understanding of God's character and His unwavering faithfulness. This difference is critical, highlighting that authentic faith demands commitment, perseverance, and an active pursuit of God's will. It's not a magic formula for avoiding hardship but a steadfast trust that enables us to navigate challenges with resilience and purpose.

The pursuit of success, guided by faith, is not about accumulating wealth or achieving worldly recognition for its own sake. Rather, it's about utilizing our talents and abilities to fulfill God's purpose, impacting the lives of others positively, and leaving a legacy that honors Him. This involves aligning our passions with His calling, understanding that the true measure of success lies in our spiritual growth and the positive impact we have on the world around us. This path may involve sacrifices and challenges, but the reward is a life filled with purpose, meaning, and a deep sense of fulfillment that transcends material gain. This perspective changes the definition of success, from a purely materialistic interpretation to a life focused on God's plan and the betterment of humanity.

Therefore, faith is not simply a belief; it is a powerful force that empowers us to overcome obstacles, pursue goals aligned with God's purpose, and achieve remarkable things. It's a journey of continuous learning, growth, and active engagement with God, marked by consistent prayer, Bible study, and a steadfast belief in His power and promises. It's the driving force behind achieving a life that is not just successful, but meaningful, fulfilling, and eternally significant. The path to biblical success, therefore, is not a solo journey, but a partnership with God, fueled by unwavering faith and a heart surrendered to His will. It is a journey of trust, perseverance, and ultimately, the profound satisfaction of living a life that honors God and impacts the world for good.

CHAPTER 5

TRUST IN GOD'S PROVIDENCE

Trusting in God's providence is not merely a passive acceptance of whatever happens; it's an active partnership with the divine, a conscious decision to surrender control and allow God to guide our steps. This isn't about relinquishing responsibility, but rather about recognizing that our plans, however meticulously crafted, are ultimately subservient to His sovereign will. Proverbs 16:9 states, "In their hearts humans plan their course, but the Lord establishes their steps." This verse beautifully encapsulates the essence of God's providence – He is not merely an observer of our lives but an active participant, shaping our paths and guiding us towards His purposes.

The concept of providence is deeply woven into the fabric of the Bible. Consider the life of David, the shepherd boy who became king. His rise to power was anything but predictable. From facing Goliath, a seemingly insurmountable challenge, to navigating political intrigue and betrayals, David's journey was fraught with peril. Yet, throughout his tumultuous life, David consistently demonstrated his trust in God's providence. He relied on God's strength in battle (1 Samuel 17), sought His guidance through prayer (Psalm 139), and acknowledged His sovereign hand even in the face of adversity (Psalm 23). David's life serves as a powerful testament to the fact that surrendering control to God does not equate to passivity; instead, it fosters an active reliance on His wisdom and strength, leading to unexpected successes that far exceed our own capabilities. His unwavering faith transformed seemingly insurmountable obstacles into stepping stones toward fulfilling God's plan for his life. Similarly, consider the story of Esther. Chosen by fate, and later by God's providence, to become queen, Esther faced a perilous situation that threatened her people. Haman, the king's chief advisor, plotted to exterminate the Jews. Esther, placed in a position of immense power and influence, could have easily retreated, prioritizing her own safety. Instead, she bravely chose to trust in God's providence, risking her own life to intercede for her people. Her courage and reliance on God's timing led to the miraculous reversal of Haman's decree, saving her people from annihilation (Esther 4-7). This powerful narrative underscores that placing our trust in God's providence doesn't necessitate a passive waiting game; it can empower us to act boldly and decisively, trusting that God will work through us to achieve His purposes.

The book of Job provides a profound exploration of trust in God's providence, albeit through a lens of immense suffering. Job, a righteous man, faced unimaginable loss and affliction, seemingly without reason. His friends offered explanations, attributing his suffering to hidden sins. Yet, Job, despite his intense suffering, maintained his faith in God's goodness and justice. He didn't fully understand God's plan, but he trusted that God had a purpose, even in his pain.

Job's unwavering faith, even in the absence of a clear explanation, stands as a powerful example of enduring trust in the face of incomprehensible hardship. Job's story teaches us that trust in God's providence is not about understanding His reasons, but about trusting His character. His faithfulness, even in the midst of unexplainable suffering, is a powerful testament to the strength that comes from surrendering to God's will. He demonstrates that true trust endures even when our understanding fails.

It's crucial to differentiate trusting in God's providence from passive resignation. Passive resignation is a fatalistic acceptance of whatever happens, without any active engagement with God or effort on our own part. It is a surrender that lacks faith and hope. Trusting in God's providence, however, involves actively seeking His guidance through prayer, studying His word, and listening for His direction. It's a dynamic interplay between faith and action, where we trust in God's plan while diligently pursuing our goals. We work hard, but we recognize that our efforts are ultimately in His hands.

Developing trust in God's providence requires a conscious effort and consistent practice. It's a journey of faith, not a destination. Here are some practical strategies for cultivating this essential aspect of faith:

Prayer:

Consistent prayer is paramount. It's not merely about asking God for things, but about developing a relationship with Him, sharing our joys and sorrows, seeking His wisdom, and surrendering our anxieties. Prayer is a two-way communication, strengthening our connection to God and deepening our trust in His care.

Bible Study:

Regular engagement with Scripture provides a rich source of inspiration and guidance. Reading stories of individuals who faced challenges and trusted in God's providence helps us understand that we are not alone in our struggles, and that God has always been faithful to those who trust in Him.

Seeking Counsel:

Surrounding ourselves with supportive faith community is vital. Seeking guidance from trusted spiritual mentors and friends can provide encouragement, accountability, and help us discern God's direction in our lives.

Journaling:

Reflecting on God's past actions in our lives can strengthen our trust. Keeping a journal where we record God's provision and guidance, large and small, helps us see patterns of His faithfulness, solidifying our confidence in His plan.

Gratitude:

Practicing gratitude helps us focus on God's blessings, fostering a sense of dependence and trust.

Actively recognizing and appreciating God's provision in our lives strengthens our faith and confirms His love and care.

The path to success, guided by God's providence, is often unpredictable and winding. There will be moments of doubt, fear, and uncertainty. Yet, by actively trusting in God's plan, surrendering control, and diligently pursuing His will, we embark on a journey filled with purpose, meaning, and ultimately, success defined by far more than material wealth. It's a journey that reveals not only God's faithfulness but also the profound strength and resilience that emerge when we place our complete trust in His loving hands. It's a journey that transforms challenges into opportunities for growth, and ultimately reveals the true meaning of a life well-lived. The true measure of success, therefore, is not found in the accumulation of riches or worldly accomplishments, but in the steadfast trust in God's plan, the unwavering faith in His promises, and the enduring commitment to a life lived in accordance with His will. This is the pathway to a life that is not only successful, but also deeply meaningful and eternally significant.

CHAPTER 6

DILIGENCE AND PERSEVERANCE KEYS TO SUCCESS

Diligence and perseverance are not merely buzzwords in the pursuit of success; they are fundamental pillars upon which lasting achievement is built. The Bible is replete with examples of individuals who, through unwavering commitment and steadfast endurance, achieved remarkable things, not solely for personal gain, but often for the greater glory of God and the betterment of others. These individuals didn't stumble upon success; they forged it through diligent effort, persistent dedication, and an unwavering faith that carried them through challenges and setbacks.

Consider the life of Joseph, whose story unfolds in the book of Genesis. Sold into slavery by his brothers, Joseph faced unimaginable hardship. Yet, rather than succumbing to despair, he displayed remarkable diligence and perseverance. He faithfully served his master, Potiphar, earning his trust and rising through the ranks. Even when falsely accused and imprisoned, Joseph didn't lose heart. He maintained his integrity, interpreting dreams with remarkable accuracy, ultimately rising to become second in command in Egypt, a position from which he saved his family and countless others from starvation. Joseph's journey is a testament to the power of unwavering commitment. His diligence in his work, even in the face of adversity, paved the way for his eventual elevation and allowed him to play a pivotal role in God's larger plan. His perseverance in the face of injustice speaks volumes to the strength one can draw upon with God's guidance.

The apostle Paul, a prominent figure in the New Testament, provides another powerful example. His life was a relentless pursuit of spreading the Gospel, despite facing relentless persecution, imprisonment, shipwrecks, and countless hardships. His unwavering commitment to his faith and his tireless efforts in evangelization led to the establishment of numerous churches and the widespread dissemination of Christianity throughout the Roman Empire. Paul's epistles, filled with profound theological insights and practical advice, are a testament to his diligence in his calling and his perseverance in the face of immense opposition. His writings demonstrate his meticulous dedication to ensuring the strength and integrity of the early church. His unrelenting work ethic serves as a powerful example of dedication to a higher calling, even amidst persistent struggles.

These biblical examples highlight a crucial truth: diligence and perseverance are not simply about working hard; they are about maintaining a focused and consistent effort toward a worthwhile goal. They entail embracing discipline, overcoming procrastination, and consistently pushing past obstacles that inevitably arise. It's about maintaining your momentum, not allowing temporary setbacks to derail your long-term vision. It's the consistent pursuit of excellence, not merely the pursuit of easy success.

The path to success, as illuminated through the lives of these biblical figures, is rarely linear. It's a winding road, punctuated by challenges, setbacks, and moments of doubt. It requires a resilience that springs from faith, a determination fueled by conviction, and a tenacity that refuses to be defeated.

This journey demands a profound understanding of oneself and one's capabilities, an awareness of potential limitations, and a commitment to constantly seeking personal growth and development.

Developing diligence and perseverance is not an innate trait; it's a skill that is cultivated and honed through consistent practice. It requires a conscious effort to prioritize tasks, manage time effectively, and cultivate self-discipline. Here are several strategies based on biblical principles that can help you foster these essential qualities:

1. Setting Realistic Goals and Breaking Down Tasks:

Proverbs 16:3 states, "Commit to the Lord whatever you do, and he will establish your plans." Before embarking on any endeavor, take time to prayerfully consider your goals. Break down large, overwhelming tasks into smaller, manageable steps. This approach prevents feelings of being overwhelmed and allows for consistent progress, fostering a sense of accomplishment that fuels further motivation. This mirrors the meticulous planning found in the construction of Solomon's Temple, a project of immense scale that was achieved through careful organization and incremental progress.

2. Cultivating Self-Discipline:

Self-discipline is the engine that drives perseverance. It's the ability to resist immediate gratification in favor of long-term goals. The book of Galatians emphasizes the importance of self-control, a key component of the fruit of the Spirit. Developing this involves cultivating habits of consistency and focus, learning to prioritize tasks, and resisting distractions. This may involve setting time limits for certain activities, minimizing interruptions, or creating a dedicated workspace conducive to focus. It's a consistent effort, mirroring the discipline of an athlete training for a significant competition.

3. Embracing Patience and Endurance:

James 1:4 reminds us, "Let perseverance finish its work so that you may be mature and complete, not lacking anything." The path to success is rarely instantaneous. It demands patience and endurance. There will be times when progress seems slow, and challenges may seem insurmountable. During such times, relying on your faith and the promise of God's guidance is crucial. Patience is not passive resignation; it's the active pursuit of a goal while acknowledging that the process requires time and effort.

4. Learning from Setbacks:

Failure is not the opposite of success; it's a stepping stone towards it. Every setback provides a valuable learning opportunity. Analyze your mistakes, identify areas for improvement, and use these experiences to refine your strategies and strengthen your resolve. This approach mirrors the many challenges faced by biblical figures such as Moses, whose leadership involved numerous setbacks and moments of self-doubt, yet through perseverance and God's guidance, led his people to freedom.

5. Surrounding Yourself with Positive Influences:

The company we keep significantly impacts our behavior and motivation. Proverbs 13:20 says, "Walk with the wise and become wise, for a companion of fools suffers harm." Seek out individuals who share your goals, support your efforts, and encourage your perseverance. Avoid those who discourage your efforts or offer negativity. A supportive community of faith can be invaluable in providing encouragement, accountability, and guidance during challenging times.

6. Practicing Gratitude:

A grateful heart is a resilient heart. Focusing on what you have achieved, instead of dwelling on what remains, fosters a positive outlook and reinforces your motivation. Expressing gratitude for God's blessings, both large and small, helps you maintain perspective and strengthens your faith.

7. Prayer and Seeking God's Guidance:

Ultimately, the pursuit of success, guided by biblical principles, should be a prayerful endeavor. Seek God's wisdom and guidance in all your decisions. Ask for strength, courage, and perseverance in overcoming obstacles. Prayer is not just a request for help; it's a strengthening of your connection to the divine source of strength and resilience.

The journey to lasting success, inspired by biblical wisdom, is not a sprint; it's a marathon. It requires consistent effort, unwavering commitment, and unyielding faith. Through diligence, perseverance, and a steadfast reliance on God's guidance, you can overcome obstacles, achieve your goals, and ultimately fulfill your God-given purpose, creating a legacy that honors Him and blesses those around you. The rewards extend far beyond material success; they encompass spiritual growth, a deeper relationship with God, and a life lived with meaning and purpose. It is in this pursuit thatn this pursuit, you will find not just success but fulfillment.

CHAPTER 7

WISDOM AND DISCERNMENT IN DECISION MAKING

The pursuit of lasting success, as previously discussed, hinges not only on diligence and perseverance but also on the crucial element of wisdom. While diligence provides the engine and perseverance the fuel, wisdom acts as the skilled navigator, guiding our efforts towards their intended destination. The Bible repeatedly emphasizes the importance of wisdom, not simply as intellectual knowledge, but as a divinely bestowed gift that empowers us to make sound judgments and navigate life's complexities with discernment and grace. It's a gift that's actively sought, cultivated, and applied. It's not merely about accumulating information; it's about understanding and applying that information in a way that honors God and benefits ourselves and others.

Proverbs, a book brimming with practical wisdom, highlights this distinction. Proverbs 1:7 states, "The fear of the Lord is the beginning of knowledge, but fools despise wisdom and instruction." This verse doesn't simply equate wisdom with knowledge; it establishes a foundational connection between the reverent fear of God and the acquisition of true wisdom. This fear is not a fearful apprehension but a deep respect and awe, a recognition of God's sovereignty and authority in all things. It is this foundational reverence that allows us to approach decisions with humility and a willingness to seek divine guidance.

Contrast this with mere intellect. Intelligence can amass facts and figures, but wisdom discerns the underlying principles, weighs potential consequences, and ultimately makes choices aligned with a greater purpose. A person can be highly intelligent, possessing a vast store of knowledge, yet lack the wisdom to apply it effectively in their life. This is akin to possessing a powerful engine in a vehicle without a skilled driver—the potential is there, but it remains untapped without the wisdom to guide it. This lack of wisdom often leads to poor decision-making, resulting in setbacks and unforeseen consequences, even with the best of intentions.

The book of James further illuminates the difference. James 1:5 says, "If any of you lacks wisdom, you should ask God, who gives generously to all without finding fault, and it will be given to you." This verse is a profound invitation, a promise from God that wisdom isn't something we must attain solely through our own efforts. It's a gift freely offered to those who humbly seek it. The act of asking demonstrates humility, a crucial component of wisdom itself. It's an acknowledgment of our limitations and a reliance on a higher power for guidance. The verse also assures us that God's gift of wisdom is not limited or withheld; it's abundant and freely given to all who ask.

Seeking wisdom is not a passive endeavor; it's an active pursuit. It involves prayerful reflection, careful consideration of available information, and a willingness to listen to counsel from trusted sources. Proverbs 15:22 states, "Without counsel, plans fail, but with many advisers they succeed." This emphasizes the importance of seeking advice and counsel from wise individuals who can provide different perspectives and insights. This doesn't imply a relinquishing of personal responsibility; instead, it recognizes the value of collaborative decision-making, leveraging the collective wisdom of others to make more informed choices. This is particularly relevant in business decisions, where seeking advice from mentors, trusted colleagues, or advisors can significantly impact the success or failure of an endeavor. In our personal lives, seeking counsel from trusted friends, family members, and spiritual mentors can provide valuable support and guidance.

Applying wisdom to career choices involves prayerful discernment. Is this career path aligned with God's plan for my life? Does it allow me to utilize my gifts and talents in a way that honors Him? Does it provide opportunities for growth, both professionally and spiritually? These are not questions easily answered, but they require thoughtful consideration and prayerful reflection. It might involve assessing the work environment, considering the potential impact on family life, and seeking guidance from individuals who have experience in the chosen field. It's about understanding not only the immediate benefits but also the long-term implications and potential challenges.

Relationships also benefit immensely from the application of wisdom. Proverbs 17:17 states, "A friend loves at all times, and a brother is born for adversity." This wisdom highlights the enduring nature of true friendship, a bond that withstands the trials and challenges of life. In applying this, we learn to cultivate relationships based on mutual respect, understanding, and commitment, even when disagreements or difficulties arise. Wisdom helps us navigate conflicts constructively, prioritizing reconciliation and understanding over contention and bitterness. It involves choosing our companions wisely, seeking those who uplift and support our spiritual growth.

Financial decisions, often fraught with complexity, also require wisdom. Proverbs 22:7 states, "The rich rule over the poor, and the borrower is servant to the lender." This verse cautions against the dangers of debt and the importance of responsible financial management. Wisdom in this area involves careful budgeting, avoiding unnecessary expenses, and making sound investment decisions. It also entails a generous spirit, recognizing the importance of giving back to others and supporting worthy causes. This isn't solely about accumulating wealth but managing resources in a way that aligns with God's principles of stewardship and generosity.

The application of wisdom is a lifelong journey, not a destination. It requires continuous learning, a willingness to adapt to changing circumstances, and a commitment to seeking God's guidance in all things. It's about embracing humility, recognizing our limitations, and relying on God's strength and wisdom to navigate the complexities of life. The path to lasting success isn't merely about accumulating wealth or achieving worldly recognition; it's about living a life of purpose, integrity, and faith, guided by the wisdom that comes from above. This wisdom, when coupled with diligence and perseverance, leads to a life that is not only successful but also deeply fulfilling and pleasing to God. It's a life characterized by sound judgment, wise decisions, and a lasting legacy built on biblical principles. This journey of cultivating wisdom is an ongoing process, requiring consistent effort, self-reflection, and a dependence on the wisdom of God. The rewards, both temporal and spiritual, are immeasurable.

CHAPTER 8

INTEGRITY BUILDING TRUST AND REPUTATION

Integrity, a cornerstone of a life well-lived, stands as a testament to the unwavering commitment to truthfulness, honesty, and moral uprightness. It's not merely the absence of wrongdoing, but the active pursuit of righteousness, a steadfast adherence to one's values even amidst adversity or temptation. The Bible abounds with examples that illuminate the importance of integrity, demonstrating its profound impact on both personal and professional success. Consider Joseph, whose unwavering commitment to his moral principles, even in the face of extreme pressure from Potiphar's wife, ultimately led to his elevation to a position of power and influence in Egypt (Genesis 39). His story serves as a potent illustration of how steadfast integrity, even amidst challenging circumstances, can pave the way for remarkable advancement.

Joseph's narrative transcends mere personal achievement; it underscores the far-reaching consequences of integrity. His refusal to compromise his values not only protected his own moral standing but also prevented a grave injustice and preserved his future potential. His story, recounted throughout generations, serves as a powerful testament to the rewards of integrity – not simply material prosperity, but a legacy of unwavering righteousness that continues to inspire. It's a compelling example of how a life anchored in integrity can lead to unintended, yet profoundly positive, outcomes.

The biblical narrative frequently emphasizes that genuine success isn't solely measured by worldly accomplishments, but also by the ethical compass guiding one's actions. Joseph's story underscores this profoundly.

Another compelling example lies in the life of Daniel, a young man exiled to Babylon, who remained steadfast in his faith and commitment to God's law despite the pervasive pagan influence around him (Daniel 1-6). His refusal to compromise his convictions, even when faced with the potential loss of his life, showcases the profound power of unwavering integrity. His steadfastness not only secured his own spiritual well-being, but it also established him as a trusted and influential figure within the Babylonian court, a testament to the potent influence of ethical conduct in even the most challenging environments. Daniel's example highlights the principle that integrity, far from being a hindrance to success, often becomes a catalyst for advancement, earning trust and respect that transcends cultural and societal boundaries. His life serves as a beacon, illuminating the pathway for success defined not by worldly ambition, but by a life lived in accordance with divine principles.

Furthermore, consider the life of David, a man chosen by God to lead Israel. While his life demonstrates both remarkable strengths and significant failings, his eventual repentance after his transgression with Bathsheba and his steadfast loyalty to God demonstrates the importance of acknowledging mistakes and striving for moral consistency (2 Samuel 12). Despite his flaws, David's sincere repentance and his determination to uphold justice and integrity, even after periods of moral failing, highlight the possibility of redemption and the ongoing pursuit of righteousness. The account of David's life, although complex, underscores the dynamic nature of character development and the persistent need for self-reflection and moral growth. His story isn't one of flawless perfection, but of striving towards moral wholeness, an ongoing journey that underscores the importance of persistent ethical commitment.

These biblical examples offer profound lessons about the practical application of integrity in various aspects of life. In the professional realm, maintaining integrity translates to honesty in dealings, fair treatment of colleagues, and ethical conduct in business practices. It means resisting the temptation to cut corners, to compromise values for short-term gains, or to engage in deceptive practices. In personal relationships, integrity fosters trust, mutual respect, and lasting bonds. It's about keeping promises, honoring commitments, and being truthful, even when it's difficult. In all aspects of life, integrity is not a mere strategy for success but a fundamental expression of our moral character and reflects our devotion to ethical conduct.

Building and maintaining integrity requires consistent effort and self-reflection. It involves regularly examining our motives, actions, and words to ensure they align with our values and principles. This process requires self-awareness, honesty, and a willingness to confront our shortcomings. It necessitates a commitment to personal growth, a continuous striving to improve our moral character and become more virtuous in our thoughts and deeds. It is a journey that requires vigilance, an ongoing commitment to self-assessment and refinement. We must actively cultivate habits that nurture ethical conduct and resist those that lead us away from moral uprightness.

Practical strategies for cultivating integrity include surrounding ourselves with people of strong moral character, actively seeking guidance and counsel from trusted mentors, and engaging in regular prayer and self-reflection. Mentorship and fellowship play vital roles in fostering moral strength.

The influence of godly advisors can be instrumental in shaping our values and guiding our decisions. Prayer provides a channel for seeking divine wisdom and strength, helping us navigate the moral complexities of life. The consistent practice of these strategies helps us develop a strong moral compass, enabling us to make choices that are both ethical and beneficial.

Furthermore, the cultivation of integrity necessitates a deep understanding of the potential consequences of compromising one's values. While short-term gains may seem appealing, the long-term repercussions of dishonesty and unethical behavior can be devastating. A single act of dishonesty can erode trust, damage reputations, and lead to lasting consequences. The biblical principle of sowing and reaping highlights this reality (Galatians 6:7-8). What we sow in terms of our actions and behavior, we will inevitably reap in the future. Therefore, cultivating integrity is not merely a moral imperative, but a strategic investment in our long-term well-being and success. Choosing integrity safeguards our reputation and our relationships, fostering trust and laying the foundation for a life characterized by lasting fulfillment.

Conversely, the benefits of upholding high moral standards are far-reaching and profound. Integrity attracts trust, respect, and lasting relationships. It builds a strong reputation, which opens doors to opportunities and creates a solid foundation for success. Individuals known for their integrity are often sought after for leadership roles, and their opinions are valued and respected. This builds a strong personal brand, creating a foundation of trust and credibility that fosters future opportunities. Beyond material rewards, however, integrity yields deep personal satisfaction, peace of mind, and a clear conscience. The confidence that comes from living in accordance with one's values is invaluable, providing inner strength and stability in the face of adversity. It also allows us to stand tall, with no need for self-justification or fear of hidden failures.

In conclusion, integrity, as a cornerstone of a life guided by biblical principles, forms the bedrock for lasting success. It's not merely an abstract ideal, but a practical strategy for navigating the complexities of life, both personally and professionally. By examining biblical examples of individuals who exemplified integrity, learning practical strategies for cultivating it, and recognizing the far-reaching benefits of upholding high moral standards, we can lay a solid foundation for a life that is not only successful, but also deeply fulfilling and pleasing to God. The pursuit of integrity is an ongoing journey of self-reflection, growth, and commitment to living a life characterized by honesty, truthfulness, and unwavering moral uprightness. This journey, though demanding, yields profound rewards, both in this life and the one to come. It's a testament to the power of living a life guided by faith and steadfast moral commitment.

CHAPTER 9

HANDLING CHALLENGES AND SETBACKS WITH FAITH

The path to success, as illuminated by scripture, is rarely a straight and effortless journey. It is often marked by unexpected detours, unforeseen obstacles, and moments of profound discouragement. Yet, it is within these very challenges that faith is tested, strengthened, and ultimately, refined. The biblical narrative abounds with examples of individuals who faced seemingly insurmountable hardships, yet persevered through unwavering faith, emerging stronger and more resilient on the other side. Understanding their experiences and applying the principles they exemplified can equip us to navigate our own trials with courage, hope, and unwavering trust in God's plan.

Consider the story of Job, a man renowned for his integrity and piety. Suddenly, his life is ravaged by catastrophic losses— his wealth, his children, and his health. Faced with unimaginable suffering, Job's friends, though well-intentioned, offered inadequate explanations for his affliction, suggesting he must have incurred divine wrath due to some hidden sin. Yet, even amidst this profound despair, Job's faith, though tested, did not waver completely. He wrestled with God, questioning the fairness of his suffering, but ultimately affirmed his faith in God's ultimate justice and wisdom (Job 1-42). Job's experience reminds us that faith is not the absence of doubt, but the persistence of hope, even in the face of overwhelming adversity. It is a testament to the strength that comes from trusting God's plan, even when we cannot comprehend it.

The Israelites' journey through the wilderness, as detailed in Exodus, provides another powerful illustration of enduring hardship with faith. Their escape from Egyptian slavery, while miraculous, was followed by years of wandering in the desert, marked by hunger, thirst, and constant threats from enemies. They faced moments of profound doubt and despair, questioning God's leadership and even contemplating returning to their former captivity. Yet, God's faithful provision, through miraculous interventions like manna from heaven and water from the rock, sustained them throughout their arduous journey. This experience demonstrates the importance of perseverance, reminding us that faith is not a passive acceptance of circumstances, but an active trust in God's provision and guidance throughout our trials. The Israelites' ultimate arrival in the Promised Land serves as a powerful symbol of the eventual triumph that can be achieved through faith, patience, and endurance.

The Apostle Paul's life serves as another powerful example of overcoming challenges through faith. He endured imprisonment, beatings, shipwreck, and constant persecution for his unwavering belief in Christ. Yet, through it all, his faith remained unshaken, even strengthening with each trial. His letters, filled with profound insights into the power of faith and endurance, provide invaluable guidance for navigating adversity (Romans 8:38-39; 2 Corinthians 4:16-18; Philippians 4:13). Paul's unwavering faith, despite the overwhelming hardships he endured, demonstrates the transformative power of faith in the face of adversity. His life serves as a beacon, illuminating the path towards resilience and hope in the darkest of times.

Developing resilience and maintaining a positive outlook in the face of hardship requires a deliberate and proactive approach. This involves cultivating several key spiritual disciplines. First, consistent prayer is paramount. It's not merely asking for solutions, but engaging in heartfelt communion with God, expressing vulnerability, and seeking His guidance and comfort. This involves a posture of dependence on God's strength, acknowledging our limitations, and trusting in His infinite capacity. Prayer isn't a magical formula, but a vital connection with the source of strength and hope.

Second, studying scripture provides a source of inspiration, encouragement, and wisdom. Reading stories of faith, perseverance, and triumph strengthens our own resolve and reminds us that we are not alone in our struggles. The Bible is replete with stories of individuals who faced adversity and emerged victorious through their faith. Meditating on these narratives provides comfort, strength, and guidance for navigating our own challenges.

Third, cultivating gratitude, even in the midst of hardship, shifts our perspective from focusing on our problems to appreciating the blessings that still remain. Focusing on what we have, instead of what we lack, shifts our mindset from despair to hope, providing a foundation for perseverance. The practice of gratitude transforms our outlook and strengthens our ability to cope with adversity.

Fourth, fostering strong relationships with fellow believers provides crucial support during times of trial. Sharing our struggles with others who understand and empathize allows us to gain strength, encouragement, and perspective. The support of a faith community provides a vital source of strength and helps us endure challenging times. Sharing burdens lightens the load and bolsters our resilience.

Fifth, practicing forgiveness is essential for healing and moving forward. Holding onto resentment and anger only hinders our ability to cope with adversity. Forgiving others, as well as ourselves, releases us from the burden of past hurts, allowing us to focus on the present and the future with renewed hope and strength. Forgiveness is not condoning wrong actions, but a release of bitterness and a path towards emotional healing.

The transformative power of challenges is often underestimated. While hardship is never pleasant, it often serves as a catalyst for growth, refinement, and spiritual maturity. Challenges force us to rely on God, strengthen our faith, and deepen our understanding of His character. They reveal our strengths and weaknesses, prompting us to seek growth in areas where we are lacking. The lessons learned during challenging times often shape our character and equip us to face future obstacles with greater wisdom and resilience. It is in the crucible of adversity that faith is tested, strengthened, and refined.

In conclusion, handling challenges and setbacks with faith requires a multifaceted approach. It involves actively cultivating spiritual disciplines, leaning on the support of fellow believers, and recognizing the transformative power of adversity. By studying the examples of biblical figures who faced hardship with unwavering faith, and by embracing the principles of prayer, scripture study, gratitude, forgiveness, and community support, we can equip ourselves to navigate life's trials with hope, resilience, and unwavering trust in God's unwavering love and plan for our lives. The journey may be arduous, but the destination, a life of faith-filled success, is worth the effort. Through unwavering trust in God and consistent application of biblical principles, we can transform setbacks into stepping stones towards lasting success, a success defined not just by material achievements, but by spiritual growth, resilience, and a life that glorifies God.

CHAPTER 10

GRATITUDE RECOGNIZING GODS' BLESSINGS

Cultivating a heart of gratitude is not merely a pleasant sentiment; it is a foundational principle for experiencing lasting success, as defined by both spiritual growth and worldly achievements. The Bible consistently emphasizes the importance of thankfulness, not as a passive acknowledgment of blessings, but as an active practice that transforms our perspectives and strengthens our faith. Psalm 100:4 declares, "Enter his gates with thanksgiving and his courts with praise; give thanks to him and praise his name." This verse doesn't merely suggest gratitude; it commands it, highlighting its centrality to a life lived in accordance with God's will.

The act of giving thanks is not simply about listing our possessions or accomplishments; it is a profound recognition of God's sovereignty and His hand in every aspect of our lives. It's acknowledging that every good gift, every opportunity, every success, and even every challenge, ultimately originates from Him (James 1:17). This understanding shifts our perspective from one of entitlement to one of humble dependence, recognizing that our success isn't solely the product of our own efforts, but a result of God's grace and guidance.

Consider the story of David, a shepherd boy who rose to become king of Israel. His life was marked by incredible challenges — battles against giants, betrayals by friends, and periods of exile and persecution. Yet, throughout his trials, David consistently expressed gratitude to God. His psalms are filled with expressions of thankfulness, even in the face of adversity. For instance, in Psalm 23, he famously proclaims, "The Lord is my shepherd; I shall not want." This statement is not a declaration of effortless prosperity, but a declaration of unwavering trust in God's provision, even amidst life's uncertainties. David's gratitude wasn't born from a life devoid of hardship, but from a deep-seated understanding of God's unwavering faithfulness. His experience demonstrates that expressing gratitude isn't simply a response to good times; it is a conscious choice that sustains faith in the midst of struggles.

Similarly, consider the Apostle Paul, who endured immense suffering for his faith. Imprisonment, beatings, and constant persecution were a part of his daily reality. Yet, his letters are replete with expressions of thankfulness. Philippians 4:11-13 beautifully illustrates this point: "I have learned to be content whatever the circumstances. I know what it is to be in need, and I know what it is to have plenty. I have learned the secret of being content in any and every situation, whether well fed or hungry, whether living in plenty or in want. I can do all this through him who gives me strength." Paul's contentment wasn't a denial of his circumstances; it was a recognition of God's sustaining grace, even in the midst of extreme hardship. This perspective of gratitude allowed him to persevere, even thrive, through unimaginable adversity.

How, then, do we practically cultivate a lifestyle of gratitude? It's not a passive state of mind, but an active, intentional practice. Here are several practical strategies:

Keep a Gratitude Journal:

Daily, take time to write down three to five things you are thankful for. These can be big things (a successful project, a healthy family) or small things (a beautiful sunset, a kind gesture from a stranger). The act of writing it down reinforces the feeling of gratitude, making it a more conscious part of your daily experience. The specificity of the entries helps to solidify the feeling of thankfulness and allows for a deeper reflection on God's blessings.

Practice Prayer of Thanksgiving:

Don't limit your prayers to requests and petitions. Spend time expressing thankfulness to God for His blessings, both big and small. This practice transforms prayer from a transactional exchange into an intimate communion of gratitude and worship. Expressing your thanks specifically helps to hone in on the details of God's provision, further deepening your appreciation.

Express Gratitude to Others:

Extending thankfulness beyond God includes showing appreciation to the people in your life. A simple "thank you" can make a world of difference. Taking the time to express gratitude to family, friends, colleagues, and even strangers, creates positive interactions and strengthens relationships. This acts as a positive feedback loop, deepening feelings of gratitude within yourself.

Focus on the Positive:

It's easy to dwell on our shortcomings and frustrations. Make a conscious effort to focus on the positive aspects of your life, your relationships, and your circumstances. Challenge negative thoughts and replace them with expressions of thankfulness. Actively choosing positivity creates a mindset receptive to experiencing and acknowledging blessings.

Count Your Blessings:

Take time to consciously reflect on all the good things in your life. Think about your health, your family, your friends, your opportunities, your skills, and your resources. This intentional inventory of blessings helps to counterbalance negativity and foster a deeper sense of appreciation. Consider the tangible and intangible aspects of your blessings; God's provision is often multifaceted and deserves to be acknowledged in its entirety. The benefits of gratitude extend far beyond a simple feeling of contentment. Studies have shown a strong correlation between gratitude and improved mental and physical health. It reduces stress, improves sleep, and even strengthens the immune system. From a spiritual perspective, gratitude deepens our relationship with God, strengthens our faith, and fosters a greater sense of peace and contentment. It allows us to see God's hand in our lives, even in the midst of difficult circumstances, and it strengthens our trust in His ultimate plan.

In the context of pursuing success, gratitude provides an essential foundation. It shifts our focus from what we lack to what we have, fostering a sense of contentment and reducing the pressure to constantly strive for more. It allows us to appreciate the journey, not just the destination, and to recognize God's hand in every step of the way. A grateful heart is a resilient heart, capable of weathering challenges and maintaining a positive outlook, even amidst adversity. It's a heart that understands that true success is not merely about accumulating wealth or achieving worldly recognition, but about living a life that glorifies God and reflects His love to those around us. By consistently practicing gratitude, we cultivate a spirit that is not only more resilient but also more receptive to God's blessings, guiding us toward a life of lasting fulfillment and success. As we consistently express our gratitude, we align ourselves with God's heart and open ourselves to receiving even more of His abundant grace. The practice of gratitude is not merely a helpful tool, but a spiritual discipline essential for a life of faith-filled success. It is a vital component in cultivating the character necessary to achieve our God-given potential and to leave a lasting legacy that reflects His glory.

CHAPTER 11

THE IMPORTANCE OF STRONG RELATIONSHIPS

The previous section explored the profound impact of gratitude on our lives, highlighting its role in fostering resilience and contentment. Building upon this foundation, we now turn to another crucial element in achieving a truly fulfilling and successful life, as defined by both spiritual and worldly measures: the cultivation of strong and positive relationships. The Bible consistently underscores the importance of community and connection, emphasizing that we are not meant to walk this journey alone. Our relationships, both personal and professional, significantly impact our emotional, mental, and spiritual well-being, ultimately shaping our ability to achieve our God-given potential and leave a lasting legacy.

Proverbs 17:17 wisely states, "A friend loves at all times, and a brother is born for adversity." This verse highlights the enduring nature of true friendship, emphasizing its unwavering support during both joyous times and challenging periods. Healthy relationships are not merely social connections; they are vital sources of encouragement, support, and accountability. They provide a safe space for vulnerability, growth, and mutual encouragement, which is crucial for navigating life's complexities. These relationships serve as a network of support, offering comfort during times of adversity and celebrating successes during periods of triumph. They are an essential component of a thriving life, mirroring God's design for us to live in the community.

Consider the life of Jesus Christ, who demonstrated the power of relationships through his interactions with his disciples. He chose a diverse group of individuals, each with their own strengths and weaknesses, and nurtured their relationships through shared experiences, teaching, and unwavering love. He didn't shy away from their imperfections; instead, he challenged them to grow and corrected their mistakes with compassion and understanding. This example highlights the transformative power of healthy relationships: the ability to foster growth, even amidst imperfections.

Jesus's relationships with his disciples weren't merely transactional; they were characterized by genuine love, empathy, and mutual respect. He invested time and energy in developing these bonds, and the result was a group of individuals who were transformed by his teachings and empowered to continue his ministry after his ascension. The close-knit community they formed laid the foundation for the early church, showcasing the profound impact that strong, Christ-centered relationships can have on furthering God's kingdom.

Furthermore, the biblical account of Ruth and Naomi portrays a powerful example of enduring friendship and loyalty. Naomi, facing hardship and loss, found solace and support in Ruth, her daughter-in-law. Ruth's unwavering devotion and loyalty to Naomi, even in the face of adversity, demonstrates the transformative power of self-sacrificial love and the strength derived from a supportive relationship. Their story reveals the resilience that stems from a deep and meaningful connection, highlighting the significant contribution of relationships to navigating challenges and finding hope during difficult times.

Beyond these illustrative biblical examples, we can identify several key principles that contribute to the cultivation of strong and healthy relationships. Open and honest communication is paramount. This involves not just expressing our thoughts and feelings clearly, but also actively listening to and understanding the perspectives of others. Ephesians 4:15 encourages us to "speak the truth in love." This means expressing our thoughts honestly but doing so in a way that is respectful, compassionate, and constructive. Harsh words, even if true, can damage relationships irreversibly.

Empathy, the ability to understand and share the feelings of others, plays a vital role in building healthy relationships. Putting ourselves in another person's shoes, understanding their experiences and perspectives, helps us respond with compassion and support. This empathy fosters mutual understanding and respect, laying the foundation for deep and lasting connections. 1 Corinthians 13:4-7 beautifully describes the nature of love, which includes patience, kindness, and the absence of envy or boasting. These qualities are fundamental building blocks for healthy, fulfilling relationships.

Forgiveness is another essential component of healthy relationships. Holding onto resentment and bitterness damages not only the relationship itself but also our own spiritual and emotional well-being. Matthew 6:14-15 teaches us to forgive others, just as God has forgiven us. This isn't about condoning harmful behavior, but rather about releasing the burden of resentment and choosing to move forward with grace. Forgiveness allows us to heal, repair broken trust, and rebuild strong relationships.

Investing quality time in our relationships is also vital. In our busy lives, it's easy to let relationships falter due to a lack of attention. Intentionally setting aside time for meaningful interaction, whether through conversations, shared activities, or simply spending quiet time together, strengthens bonds and deepens connections. This dedicated time fosters genuine connection and enhances the overall quality of the relationship.

Setting healthy boundaries is another crucial aspect of maintaining strong relationships. This involves establishing clear expectations and limits to protect our emotional and spiritual well-being. Healthy boundaries help to prevent unhealthy codependency and ensure that relationships remain mutually respectful and supportive. We need to protect ourselves from those who would drain our energy or manipulate us, recognizing that setting boundaries is a form of self-care that strengthens our relationships in the long run.

Active participation in a community, whether through a church, a volunteer organization, or a social group, is another pathway towards fostering fulfilling relationships. Engaging in shared activities, serving others, and building bonds with like-minded individuals enriches our lives and expands our support network. This participation strengthens our sense of belonging, combatting feelings of isolation and loneliness, and creating opportunities for meaningful interaction and growth.

Furthermore, actively seeking mentorship and offering guidance to others can greatly enrich our relationships. Mentorship provides a framework for mutual learning and growth, fostering a deeper connection between mentor and mentee. Similarly, offering guidance and support to others extends our influence positively, strengthening relationships and contributing to a sense of purpose.

In conclusion, strong and healthy relationships are not merely a desirable outcome; they are a vital component of a fulfilling and successful life, mirroring God's design for humanity to thrive in the community. By prioritizing open communication, empathy, forgiveness, quality time, healthy boundaries, and active community involvement, we can cultivate relationships that provide unwavering support, encouragement, and a sense of belonging. As we nurture these relationships, we are not only enriching our own lives but also contributing to a world that reflects God's love and compassion. The principles outlined here provide a practical framework for building strong relationships rooted in faith and reflecting the teachings of scripture, contributing to a life of lasting fulfillment and success. The cultivation of healthy relationships is a continuous process, requiring ongoing effort, commitment, and a willingness to learn and grow together. It's a journey of mutual respect, support, and love, leading to a richer, more meaningful life lived in accordance with God's plan. As we invest in our relationships, we invest in ourselves and in the future, leaving a positive legacy that honors God and blesses others.

CHAPTER 12

GENEROSITY AND GIVING BACK TO OTHERS

Building upon the foundation of strong relationships, we now delve into another crucial aspect of a fulfilling and successful life – generosity and giving back to others. The Bible consistently champions generosity, not merely as an act of charity but as a fundamental principle interwoven with faith, impacting our spiritual growth and leaving a lasting legacy. It's a testament to a heart aligned with God's, reflecting His abundant nature and fostering a life rich in blessings.

The concept of generosity transcends mere monetary contributions. It encompasses a broad spectrum of acts, from offering a kind word to extending a helping hand, from volunteering time to sharing resources. It's about a willingness to give freely, without expecting anything in return, reflecting the selfless love of Christ. 2 Corinthians 9:7 states, "Each of you should give what you have decided in your heart to give, not reluctantly or under compulsion, for God loves a cheerful giver." This verse underscores the importance of giving from the heart, highlighting the intrinsic joy derived from selfless acts. A reluctant or forced act of generosity lacks the genuine spirit of giving that God desires.

Throughout scripture, we encounter numerous examples of generous individuals whose lives were profoundly impacted by their willingness to give. Abraham, known for his unwavering faith, demonstrated remarkable generosity in offering his son Isaac as a sacrifice to God (Genesis 22). While ultimately spared, his willingness to give his most precious possession speaks volumes about his unwavering devotion and the transformative power of self-sacrificial giving. This act, though extreme, illustrates a level of devotion that translates to a willingness to sacrifice for the greater good, a principle that resonates through all aspects of a generous life.

Similarly, Joseph, despite facing immense hardship and betrayal, displayed remarkable generosity towards his brothers, who had previously wronged him (Genesis 50). He forgave their actions and provided for them during a time of famine, demonstrating a capacity for grace and compassion that transcended personal hurt. His forgiveness and generosity not only restored his relationship with his brothers but also preserved his family, and the future generations. This forgiveness speaks volumes about the transformative potential of generous acts. It wasn't just material support; it was emotional healing and the restoring of familial bonds, demonstrating a deeper level of generosity that transforms both the giver and the receiver.

Consider the parable of the Good Samaritan (Luke 10:25-37). This story is not just an illustration of generosity; it's a profound lesson on compassion and extending kindness to those outside our immediate circles. The Samaritan, despite societal prejudice, showed immense compassion and generosity to the injured man, a stranger, providing aid and care. The parable highlights that true generosity extends beyond our comfort zones, challenging us to embrace those who may be different or marginalized. The Samaritan's actions weren't motivated by the expectation of reward; it was pure compassion and a demonstration of God's love in action. The impact of his generous act transcended a simple act of aid, becoming a lasting symbol of extending grace to those in need, highlighting the far-reaching consequences of a generous act.

These biblical examples are not just historical accounts; they are living testaments to the transformative power of generosity. They demonstrate that giving is not about diminishing ourselves; it's about enriching our lives and the lives of others. Generosity cultivates a sense of purpose, fosters deeper connections with others, and opens us to God's blessings in unexpected ways. It aligns our hearts with God's, reflecting His boundless love and abundance.

The principle of generosity extends beyond financial contributions. Time, talent, and skills are equally valuable assets that can be generously offered to others. Volunteering at a local charity, mentoring a young person, or sharing our expertise with someone in need are all expressions of generosity that can have a profound impact. Proverbs 11:25 states, "A generous person will prosper; whoever refreshes others will be refreshed." This verse underscores the reciprocal nature of generosity, suggesting that giving not only benefitsbenefits not only the recipient but also the giver, leading to personal enrichment and prosperity.

Practical strategies for incorporating generosity into our lives are numerous. First, we can begin by assessing our resources, both material and non-material. This involves honest self-reflection, and identifying areas where we can offer others assistance, time, skills, or talents to others. Creating a budget that allocates a portion of our income to charitable giving can help formalize our commitment. Moreover, considering a regular, consistent pattern of giving rather than sporadic contributions fosters a habit of generosity that becomes a natural part of our lifestyle.

Second, we can seek opportunities to serve others within our communities. This could involve volunteering at a local soup kitchen, working at a homeless shelter, or assisting the elderly with chores. These acts of service not only benefit the recipients but also deepen our understanding of the needs within our community. We can identify organizations aligned with our values and commit to supporting them regularly. This commitment strengthens our ties to the community and broadens our perspectives, enhancing our sense of belonging and purpose.

Third, we can identify our specific skills and talents and look for ways to use them to serve others. Are you a skilled teacher? Offer tutoring services to underprivileged children. Are you a talented musician? Perform at a charity event. Are you a gifted writer? Volunteer to write grant proposals for a non-profit. Identifying and utilizing our talents in service to others enhances both our self-worth and the well-being of others, demonstrating a deeper form of generosity.

Fourth, we must cultivate an attitude of gratitude. Gratitude opens our hearts to recognize the blessings in our lives, inspiring us to share those blessings with others. Focusing on what we have rather than what we lack fosters a spirit of thankfulness that naturally leads to generosity and a desire to give back. Practicing gratitude daily, through journaling or prayer, cultivates a heart that's open to the blessings of giving.

Finally, we need to consciously make giving a priority, integrating it into our daily routines. Just as we prioritize other important aspects of our lives, making time for generous acts should also be a non-negotiable part of our schedule. This prioritization ensures that generosity is not just a sporadic activity but a consistent commitment that permeates our lives.

Generosity isn't merely a religious act; it's a powerful catalyst for personal transformation and societal betterment. By embracing the principles of generosity, we move beyond self-centeredness and embrace a life of purpose, leaving a legacy of kindness, compassion, and love. This journey of giving back is a continuous process, a lifelong commitment to reflecting God's love and grace in our actions. As we dedicate ourselves to a life of generosity, we discover that the greatest rewards are not material possessions, but the profound sense of fulfillment, the strengthened relationships, and the enduring legacy of positive impact on the lives of others. This is a pathway to a truly successful life, measured not just by worldly achievements but by the richness of our contributions to the world around us. The true measure of success lies in the lives we touch, the hearts we inspire, and the legacy of love and generosity we leave behind.

CHAPTER 13

MENTORSHIP AND DISCIPLESHIP GUIDING OTHERS

Building on the principles of generosity and giving, we now turn our attention to another vital aspect of leaving a lasting legacy: mentorship and discipleship. These intertwined concepts are not merely about imparting knowledge or skills; they represent a profound commitment to nurturing spiritual growth, fostering personal development, and guiding others towards a life of purpose and success, as defined by biblical principles. The Bible is replete with examples of mentorship and discipleship, highlighting their transformative power in shaping lives and leaving an enduring impact.

Consider the relationship between Elijah and Elisha. Elijah, a powerful prophet, didn't merely instruct Elisha; he actively invested in him, allowing Elisha to witness his miracles and learn through observation and practical application. Elisha, in turn, demonstrated unwavering loyalty and commitment, faithfully following Elijah and carrying on his prophetic ministry after his ascension (2 Kings 2). This mentorship wasn't a one-time event; it was a continuous process of learning, guidance, and mutual growth. Elijah's mentoring didn't just equip Elisha with prophetic skills; it fostered a deep spiritual connection, shaping his character and preparing him for his future calling. Elisha's unwavering devotion to his mentor, and his willingness to learn and serve, reflects the essential components of a successful discipleship relationship. The lasting impact of this mentorship is evident in Elisha's subsequent ministry and legacy.

The relationship between Jesus and his disciples offers the most profound example of mentorship and discipleship. Jesus didn't just preach; he lived out his teachings, providing a living example of faith, love, and service. He invested time and energy in his disciples, patiently teaching them, correcting their mistakes, and guiding them in their spiritual development. His disciples, in turn, followed him, learned from him, and ultimately continued his ministry after his ascension. The Gospels are filled with accounts of Jesus's interactions with his disciples, revealing the intimacy, trust, and mutual respect that characterized their relationship. This wasn't a distant, formal instruction; it was a deeply personal investment in their spiritual growth, shaping them into leaders capable of carrying on His mission.

The disciples' journeys were not without challenges. They faced moments of doubt, fear, and even betrayal. Yet, Jesus's consistent guidance and unwavering support enabled them to overcome these obstacles and ultimately become the pillars of the early Christian church. The disciples' subsequent ministry, their unwavering commitment to spreading the gospel despite adversity, demonstrates the enduring power of Jesus's mentorship. Their experiences highlight that discipleship is a challenging but rewarding journey, marked by both triumphs and trials, but ultimately leading to spiritual maturity and a lasting impact on the world.

The biblical examples demonstrate that mentorship and discipleship are not hierarchical, power-driven relationships; rather, they are based on mutual respect, love, and a shared commitment to spiritual growth. The mentor provides guidance, support, and encouragement, while the disciple exhibits dedication, loyalty, and a willingness to learn. The relationship is reciprocal, with both parties benefiting from the exchange of knowledge, experience, and spiritual insight. The mentor gains the satisfaction of empowering others and witnessing their growth, while the disciple benefits from the wisdom, experience, and support of the mentor. Becoming a mentor involves several key steps. First, identify your strengths and areas of expertise. What skills, knowledge, or experiences can you share with others? This self-assessment is crucial in determining where you can most effectively contribute to the lives of others. Second, cultivate a spirit of humility and patience. Mentoring is not about self-promotion; it's about empowering others. Patience and understanding are essential in guiding individuals through their challenges and growth processes. Third, actively seek opportunities to mentor. This could involve volunteering to mentor young people in your church, community, or workplace. It could also involve offering guidance and support to individuals within your professional network. The key is to proactively create opportunities to share your knowledge and experience.

Finding a mentor requires proactive steps as well. First, identify individuals you admire and respect. These individuals could be people in your church, workplace, or community who embody the qualities and values you aspire to. Second, reach out to these individuals and express your desire for mentorship. Don't be afraid to be direct and express your admiration for their work and your desire to learn from their experience. Third, be prepared to invest time and effort in the relationship. Mentorship is a two-way street; both parties need to commit to making the relationship successful.

Beyond skill development, mentorship and discipleship encompass spiritual guidance. Mentors offer not only practical advice but also spiritual support, helping disciples navigate life's challenges with faith and trust in God. Mentorship becomes a spiritual partnership, a shared journey of faith, strengthening the bond between mentor and mentee and fostering deeper spiritual understanding. This spiritual dimension is critical, weaving faith into the core of the mentorship relationship, and providing a solid foundation for growth in all aspects of life. Prayer, shared Bible study, and mutual accountability are essential components of a faith-based mentorship, reinforcing the spiritual foundation of the relationship and fostering a deeper connection with God.

The benefits of mentorship and discipleship extend beyond personal growth. They create a ripple effect, influencing future generations and leaving a lasting legacy of faith, wisdom, and service. Mentors become catalysts for positive change, empowering individuals to achieve their potential and contribute meaningfully to society. The disciples, in turn, become mentors themselves, passing on the wisdom and knowledge they have received, perpetuating a cycle of growth and empowerment that impacts generations to come. This continuity of mentorship is vital in preserving and extending the principles of faith and service within communities and across generations.

In conclusion, mentorship and discipleship are vital components of a life guided by faith and striving for success, as defined by biblical principles. By embracing these concepts, we not only contribute to the growth of others but also enrich our own lives, forging lasting relationships and leaving a legacy that extends far beyond our own lifetimes. The act of mentoring or being mentored is a journey of mutual benefit, reinforcing faith, fostering personal growth, and extending God's love and grace to others. The legacy of a life invested in mentoring and discipleship is one of profound impact and enduring blessing. The richness of this legacy extends beyond material gains, reaching the realm of spiritual enrichment and a lasting contribution to the Kingdom of God.

CHAPTER 14

LEAVING A POSITIVE LEGACY FOR FUTURE GENERATIONS

Leaving a positive legacy isn't about achieving fame or fortune; it's about making a difference that resonates through time, a testament to a life lived purposefully and in accordance with God's design. The Bible is filled with examples of individuals who, through their actions and faith, left an indelible mark on subsequent generations. Consider Abraham, the father of faith. His unwavering obedience to God, despite facing seemingly insurmountable challenges, laid the foundation for the nation of Israel and the lineage of Christ. His legacy isn't simply a historical record; it's a living testament to the power of faith and unwavering trust in God's promises (Genesis 12-25). Abraham's legacy extends far beyond his immediate family; it encompasses the entire Judeo-Christian tradition, impacting billions of lives across millennia. His life serves as a constant reminder that a life lived in devotion to God echoes through history.

Similarly, Moses, the liberator of Israel, left a legacy that transcends his own lifetime. His leadership, courage, and unwavering faith in God's power delivered the Israelites from slavery in Egypt. More significantly, he received the Ten Commandments, providing a moral and legal framework that has guided societies for centuries (Exodus 1-40). Moses's legacy isn't limited to the legal code; it extends to the profound impact on the development of ethical and spiritual principles in Western civilizations. His steadfastness in the face of adversity and his humility despite possessing immense powerDespite his immense power, his steadfastness in the face of adversity and his humility stand as enduring examples of righteous leadership and unwavering faith. David, the shepherd boy who became king, offers another profound illustration. Despite his flaws and struggles, David's deep faith in God, his unwavering commitment to His people, and his profound capacity for repentance shaped his legacy (1 Samuel 16-1 Kings 2). His psalms, expressions of his deep devotion and intimate relationship with God, continue to inspire and comfort people worldwide. David's legacy isn't just about his kingship or his military prowess; it's about the enduring influence of his spiritual writings and the impact of his repentance on his life and subsequent leadership. The psalm's ability to resonate across cultures and generations highlights the enduring power of faith, devotion, and the transformative impact of repentance.

These biblical figures didn't achieve their legacies through extraordinary circumstances; rather, they demonstrated ordinary virtues – faith, obedience, humility, perseverance, and compassion – with extraordinary consistency. Their lives were woven with the thread of faith, each action reflecting a commitment to God's plan. Their lasting impact is not a result of chance or luck, but the fruit of a life lived purposefully in accordance with God's will.

Building a lasting positive legacy involves a conscious and intentional approach, a deliberate shaping of our lives to reflect God's character and purpose. It's not a passive process but an active engagement in shaping our future and the future of generations to come. This requires a multifaceted approach, encompassing personal development, professional endeavors, and community involvement.

On a personal level, cultivating virtues such as integrity, honesty, compassion, and humility is paramount. Integrity, as demonstrated by Joseph in the face of temptation (Genesis 39), reflects unwavering adherence to moral principles, even under pressure. Honesty, like the truthfulness of Nathan in confronting David (2 Samuel 12), builds trust and strengthens relationships. Compassion, exemplified by Jesus in his ministry (Matthew 25), fosters empathy and understanding. Humility, evident in the example of Jesus washing the disciples' feet (John 13), prevents arrogance and fosters self-awareness. These virtues, consistently demonstrated, shape character and influence the lives of others, creating a ripple effect that extends beyond immediate circles.

Professionally, our legacy is shaped by our commitment to excellence, ethical conduct, and service. Striving for excellence, not merely for personal gain but for contributing meaningful work to society, reflects a commitment to using our skills and talents for God's glory (Colossians 3:23). Maintaining ethical conduct, even when faced with temptations or pressure to compromise, builds trust and reinforces integrity (Proverbs 11:3). Contributing to society through our professional endeavors, going beyond the minimum requirements and actively seeking opportunities to make a positive impact, resonates through our work and inspires others.

Beyond personal and professional spheres, building a lasting legacy involves contributing to our communities and leaving the world a better place than we found it. Volunteering time and resources to causes aligned with our faith and values, actively engaging in our local churches and communities, and supporting organizations that alleviate suffering and promote justice all contribute to this vision. These acts of service, fueled by faith and a sense of responsibility towards others, are powerful expressions of our commitment to making a positive difference.

The Bible underscores the lasting impact of living a virtuous life. Proverbs 10:7 states, "The memory of the righteous is blessed," indicating that the actions and character of those who live righteously leave an enduring legacy that is remembered and celebrated. This lasting impact isn't merely a matter of reputation; it speaks to the ripple effect of virtuous living, influencing subsequent generations and shaping a better future.

Furthermore, the concept of "planting seeds" is used extensively in scripture to depict the lasting impact of actions, both positive and negative. Galatians 6:7-8 reminds us that we will reap what we sow. This principle extends beyond immediate consequences; the seeds we plant, through our words, actions, and choices, shape the landscape of future generations. The legacy we leave is a direct reflection of the seeds we have sown throughout our lives. A life dedicated to faith, virtue, and service plants seeds of positive change that will bear fruit long after we are gone. The legacy is not just about what we leave behind materially; it's about the intangible imprint we leave on the hearts and minds of others, a lasting impact that inspires and uplifts generations to come. This legacy is a testament to a life lived not just for ourselves, but for God's glory and the betterment of humanity, a legacy that continues to inspire and encourage others in their journey of faith and purpose. Our lives, therefore, are not merely temporal events; they are the building blocks of a lasting legacy, a contribution to the ongoing narrative of God's plan for humanity. This legacy transcends earthly limitations, extending into eternity, and reflects the impact of a life lived in harmony with God's purpose.

CHAPTER 15

LIVING A LIFE THAT HONORS GOD

Living a life that honors God isn't merely about adhering to a set of rules; it's about cultivating a deep and abiding relationship with Him, allowing His love to transform our hearts and shape our actions. This transformation is not a passive process but an active engagement with God's word and a conscious effort to align our lives with His will. The Bible repeatedly emphasizes the importance of seeking God's guidance in every aspect of our lives, from the mundane to the momentous. Proverbs 3:5-6 encourages us to "Trust in the Lord with all your heart and lean not on your own understanding; in all your ways submit to him, and he will make your paths straight." This verse encapsulates the essence of a life lived in accordance with God's will: a life characterized by trust, submission, and a reliance on God's wisdom rather than our own limited understanding.

This trust isn't a blind faith; it's a faith grounded in the knowledge of God's character, His promises, and His unwavering love. It involves actively studying His word, praying for guidance, and seeking His will in every decision we make. This active engagement with God fosters a deep sense of connection and reliance, enabling us to navigate life's challenges with confidence and grace. When we make decisions based on our own desires or ambitions, we risk straying from God's path, compromising our integrity, and ultimately hindering our personal growth and fulfillment.

But when we seek God's guidance, we open ourselves to His wisdom, His protection, and His abundant blessings.

The pursuit of righteousness, therefore, isn't a burden but a privilege. It's an opportunity to partner with God in fulfilling His purposes and experiencing the fullness of life He offers. This pursuit involves a constant striving to live in accordance with God's teachings, emulating His character, and reflecting His love to the world around us. It demands a commitment to integrity, honesty, compassion, and humility, the very qualities that characterized the life of Jesus Christ, our ultimate example. His life serves as a beacon, guiding us on the path towards a life that honors God and leaves a lasting legacy.

Practical strategies for integrating faith into daily life are crucial in this pursuit. These strategies aren't complex or esoteric rituals; they're simple, everyday actions that reflect a commitment to living a life pleasing to God. One essential practice is consistent prayer. Prayer isn't merely a request for blessings; it's a conversation with God, a time to express gratitude, confess our sins, seek His wisdom, and surrender our lives to His will. Through prayer, we cultivate intimacy with God, allowing Him to shape our thoughts, feelings, and actions. Regular prayer strengthens our relationship with God and empowers us to overcome challenges with His strength and guidance.

Another essential practice is daily Bible study. The Bible is not merely a historical document; it's a living word, offering guidance, wisdom, and inspiration for every aspect of our lives. Regularly reading and studying the scriptures helps us understand God's character, His plans for our lives, and His expectations for us. It provides context for our challenges, offering comfort, hope, and a blueprint for living a righteous life. The study should not be merely a passive reading but an active engagement, seeking to understand the deeper meaning and application to our current situations. This active engagement brings a new light and depth to our understanding of God and his will for us.

Furthermore, engaging in acts of service is integral to living a life that honors God. Jesus commanded us to love our neighbors as ourselves, and this love is expressed through acts of kindness, compassion, and generosity. Serving others, whether through volunteering at a local charity, helping a neighbor in need, or simply offering a kind word, is a powerful way to reflect God's love and make a positive impact on the world. Such acts of service are not merely acts of charity; they are opportunities to extend God's grace and to share His love with those around us. This also acts as a vital catalyst in strengthening our relationship with God and the community.

Making ethical choices is paramount in living a life that honors God. This isn't about adhering to a rigid set of rules; it's about making decisions based on God's principles of love, justice, and righteousness. It means choosing honesty over deception, compassion over selfishness, and integrity over compromise. This requires a constant awareness of our actions and motivations, seeking God's guidance in navigating moral dilemmas and situations where ethical considerations are paramount. Every action is an opportunity to reflect God's character and honor His name.

The importance of spiritual discipline cannot be overstated. Just as physical fitness requires regular exercise, spiritual growth requires intentional practice. This involves cultivating habits that nurture our spiritual lives, such as consistent prayer, Bible study, fasting, meditation, and fellowship with other believers. Spiritual disciplines help us draw closer to God, deepen our faith, and cultivate a deeper understanding of His will for our lives. They also strengthen our resilience and ability to overcome challenges through unwavering faith in God's plans.

Beyond these personal practices, living a life that honors God involves extending our influence to our family, friends, workplace, and community. We are called to be ambassadors for Christ, reflecting His love and compassion in all our interactions. This means treating others with respect, dignity, and kindness, regardless of their beliefs or backgrounds. It involves seeking opportunities to share our faith with others, not through forceful proselytizing but through the example of our lives and the witness of our love. This outward projection of faith significantly impacts the lives of others and strengthens our own faith.

The pursuit of a life that honors God is not a solitary journey; it's a communal endeavor. Connecting with a supportive Christian community, whether through a local church or a fellowship group, is essential for spiritual growth and encouragement. Fellowship with other believers provides accountability, support, and opportunities to share our faith and encourage one another in our walk with God. This shared journey helps us to better understand the principles of faith and strengthens our own commitment to the path.

Furthermore, acknowledging our imperfections and seeking God's forgiveness is crucial in this process. We all fall short of God's standards, and it's in acknowledging these shortcomings and seeking His forgiveness that we experience the transformative power of His grace. This involves not only confessing our sins but actively seeking to change our behavior and live in accordance with His will. God's love and forgiveness offer us a chance to start anew and continue our journey of growing closer to him.

In conclusion, living a life that honors God is a journey of faith, surrender, and transformation. It's a process of actively seeking His will, aligning our lives with His principles, and reflecting His love to the world around us. This journey isn't about achieving perfection; it's about striving for holiness, seeking His guidance in every decision, and relying on His strength to overcome challenges. This commitment yields a life of purpose, fulfillment, and a lasting legacy that extends beyond our mortal lives. The path may be challenging, but the reward—a life lived in harmony with God's purpose and a legacy that reflects His glory—is immeasurable.

CHAPTER 16

APPLYING BIBLICAL WISDOM TO FINANCES

Having established the foundational principles of faith, trust, and obedience to God, we now turn to a crucial area of practical application: our finances. The Bible doesn't shy away from addressing the material aspects of life; rather, it provides a framework for managing our resources in a way that honors God and blesses others. This isn't about accumulating wealth for its own sake, but about using our resources wisely, responsibly, and generously. The scriptures offer profound wisdom on stewardship, a concept that underpins our entire approach to finances.

The parable of the talents (Matthew 25:14-30) illustrates this perfectly. The master entrusts different amounts of talents (representing abilities and resources) to his servants. Those who diligently use their talents, multiplying them through wise investment and hard work, are commended and rewarded. Conversely, the servant who buries his talent, failing to utilize the gift entrusted to him, is condemned for his inaction. This parable isn't just about money; it's about how we use all our God-given gifts and abilities—our time, talents, and resources—to further His kingdom. In the context of finances, this means being good stewards of the money God has entrusted to us. This isn't about strict frugality for its own sake, but about responsible management, mindful spending, and strategic planning.

A key aspect of biblical stewardship is saving. Proverbs 21:20 states, "The wise store up choice food and olive oil, but fools gulp theirs down." Saving isn't about hoarding wealth; it's about preparing for the future, providing for unforeseen circumstances, and having the resources to invest wisely or give generously. It requires discipline, planning, and a long-term perspective. Creating a realistic budget is crucial in achieving this. Tracking income and expenses, identifying areas where spending can be reduced, and setting aside a portion of each paycheck for savings are essential steps. This disciplined approach isn't just about financial security; it reflects a responsible approach to the resources God has provided. The goal isn't to deprive ourselves, but to manage our resources effectively and ensure financial stability.

Furthermore, the Bible emphasizes the importance of giving. 2 Corinthians 9:7 reminds us, "Each of you should give what you have decided in your heart to give, not reluctantly or under compulsion, for God loves a cheerful giver." Giving isn't just about donating to charity; it's an act of worship, expressing our gratitude for God's blessings and demonstrating our commitment to His kingdom. It's a crucial aspect of responsible stewardship, recognizing that all we have comes from God and should be used for His glory and the benefit of others. This giving should be proportionate to our income and done willingly, reflecting a heart of gratitude. Regular giving, whether to a church, a charity, or an individual in need, is a vital expression of our faith. Tithe, traditionally 10% of one's income, is often cited in scripture as a way to honor God with our first fruits. This act reflects a commitment to recognizing God as the source of all blessings.

The Bible strongly cautions against debt. Proverbs 22:7 warns, "The rich rule over the poor, and the borrower is servant to the lender." While some debt, like a mortgage for a home, may be unavoidable, the scriptures generally advise against accumulating excessive debt. This is not a call for complete financial isolation, but a caution against living beyond our means and becoming enslaved to financial obligations. Debt can lead to stress, anxiety, and financial instability, hindering our ability to serve God and others effectively. Careful budgeting, avoiding unnecessary expenses, and prioritizing needs over wants are crucial steps to avoiding debt or managing existing debt responsibly. Open communication with lenders, seeking counsel for debt consolidation, and carefully managing credit are essential steps for financial health.

Investing is another critical aspect of managing finances according to biblical principles. While the Bible doesn't offer specific investment strategies, the principles of wisdom, diligence, and prudence apply equally to financial investments as they do to other aspects of life. This involves thorough research, careful consideration of risk, and seeking advice from trusted financial professionals. Investing wisely allows for long-term growth and provides a means to achieve financial goals, support family needs, or support charitable causes. It's an extension of responsible stewardship, using our resources to generate further opportunities for growth and service. However, it is essential to avoid speculative investments driven by greed or the pursuit of quick riches, which are contrary to biblical principles of contentment and responsible stewardship.

Contentment is a vital element of a biblically sound financial approach. Philippians 4:11-13 states, "I have learned to be content whatever the circumstances. I know what it is to be in need, and I know what it is to have plenty. I have learned the secret of being content in any and every situation, whether well fed or hungry, whether living in plenty or in want." Contentment doesn't mean rejecting financial security or avoiding efforts to improve our financial standing, but it means finding joy and fulfillment in God's provision, regardless of our material possessions. This perspective frees us from the relentless pursuit of wealth, enabling us to focus on what truly matters: our relationship with God, our family, and our service to others. This contentment is not passive resignation; it is a deep-seated trust in God's provision and grace.

Conversely, the Bible strongly warns against greed. 1 Timothy 6:10 cautions, "For the love of money is the root of all kinds of evil. Some people, eager for money, have wandered from the faith and pierced themselves with many griefs." Greed is an insatiable desire for more, a focus on material possessions that overshadows our relationship with God and our commitment to serving others. It can lead to unethical behavior, compromised integrity, and a distorted sense of values. Avoiding greed requires a constant self-assessment, a commitment to contentment, and a renewed focus on the true values that God emphasizes.

Financial planning is essential in securing long-term financial stability. This involves setting long-term goals, creating a budget, managing debt, saving regularly, and investing wisely. It requires a proactive and disciplined approach, recognizing that our financial health impacts many aspects of our lives. Regular reviews of the financial plan, adjustments based on changing circumstances, and seeking advice from financial professionals as needed are all part of a comprehensive approach. This isn't a rigid, inflexible system, but a dynamic process that adapts to life's evolving challenges and opportunities.

In conclusion, applying biblical wisdom to our finances isn't about following rigid rules; it's about cultivating a heart of stewardship, gratitude, and contentment. It's about using our resources wisely, responsibly, and generously, aligning our financial practices with our faith. This approach leads not only to financial stability but also to a life that honors God and blesses others, reflecting a life lived in accordance with His principles. It's a journey of faith, requiring consistent effort, prayerful consideration, and a commitment to living a life that reflects the values and teachings found within scripture. By integrating these principles into our daily lives, we can experience the peace, purpose, and abundance that comes from aligning our finances with God's will.

CHAPTER 17

INTEGRATING FAITH IN CAREER AND WORK

Building upon the principles of financial stewardship discussed earlier, we now consider the equally vital application of faith within our careers and professional lives. The Bible doesn't offer a blueprint for specific professions, but it does provide timeless principles that guide us towards fulfilling and meaningful work, irrespective of our chosen field. These principles empower us to approach our careers not merely as a means to an end, but as an integral part of our spiritual journey, a platform for serving God and impacting others.

Diligence, a recurring theme in scripture, is paramount in our professional lives. Proverbs 10:4 states, "Lazy hands make for poverty, but diligent hands bring wealth." This isn't solely about material wealth, but about the intrinsic reward of a job well done, reflecting God's own meticulous craftsmanship in creation. Diligence manifests in several ways: consistent effort, meticulous attention to detail, punctuality, and a proactive approach to our tasks. It's about more than just fulfilling minimum requirements; it's about exceeding expectations, taking initiative, and consistently striving for excellence. This diligent approach is not only beneficial professionally, but it also cultivates a sense of accomplishment and self-respect, reflecting God's intention for us to be productive and purposeful. Imagine a craftsman meticulously shaping wood into a beautiful piece of furniture; their diligence is evident in the quality and detail of the finished product. That same dedication to craftsmanship can be applied to any vocation, regardless of its perceived importance.

Integrity is another cornerstone principle, crucial for navigating the complexities of the modern workplace. Proverbs 11:3 assures us, "The integrity of the upright guides them, but the unfaithfulness of the treacherous destroys them." Maintaining ethical standards, honesty, and transparency in our professional dealings is not merely a moral imperative but a crucial element of building trust, fostering positive relationships, and creating a thriving work environment. This resonates deeply with the biblical emphasis on truthfulness and righteousness. Compromising our integrity for personal gain or to please superiors undermines our spiritual walk and ultimately harms ourselves and those around us. Examples abound in history and current events where individuals compromised integrity and faced devastating consequences, both professionally and personally. The long-term rewards of integrity far outweigh any short-term gains from dishonest or unethical behavior.

Service, a core tenet of Christian faith, finds profound application in our professional lives. Matthew 20:26-28 states, "Whoever wants to become great among you must be your servant, and whoever wants to be first must be slave of all. For even the Son of Man did not come to be served, but to serve, and to give his life as a ransom for many." This calls us to view our work not simply as a means of self-advancement, but as an opportunity to serve our colleagues, clients, and the wider community. Whether we are teachers, doctors, entrepreneurs, or laborers, we have the opportunity to use our skills and talents to uplift others, contribute to the common good, and reflect Christ's love through our actions.

This service mentality shifts our perspective from self-centered ambition to selfless contribution, fostering a sense of purpose and fulfillment far beyond the confines of our job description. Consider a nurse tending to patients with unwavering compassion or a teacher inspiring students to reach their full potential. These acts of service illustrate how our professions can become platforms for profound impact.

Finding fulfilling work that aligns with our values requires careful consideration and prayerful reflection. This involves identifying our gifts and talents, exploring career paths that leverage those strengths, and seeking God's guidance in discerning our purpose. It may entail pursuing further education, developing new skills, or making a career change altogether. The process may involve a degree of uncertainty, but trust in God's plan and unwavering prayer can provide clarity and direction. This process should involve honestly assessing our strengths and weaknesses, seeking advice from trusted mentors, and researching various career options that align with our spiritual values. It's a journey of self-discovery, guided by faith and informed by prayer.

Furthermore, the potential for spiritual growth within a professional setting is significant. Our workplaces are often microcosms of society, providing opportunities to practice patience, forgiveness, compassion, and love in the face of adversity. Navigating conflict, handling difficult personalities, and maintaining a positive attitude even in challenging circumstances are all opportunities for spiritual growth. These experiences often shape our character and deepen our faith as we learn to apply biblical principles in the daily grind. The workplace presents countless opportunities to exercise virtues such as patience, perseverance, and humility. Conflicts with colleagues or difficult projects can challenge our faith and patience but can also lead to spiritual growth if we respond with grace and forgiveness.

Maintaining ethical standards in the workplace is essential. This includes honest work, respectful communication, and fair treatment of colleagues. Resisting the temptation to cut corners, to engage in gossip or office politics, and to compromise our values for personal gain is crucial for maintaining integrity. It is a daily demonstration of our faith and commitment to righteous living. This commitment requires vigilance, prayerful discernment, and a steadfast commitment to biblical principles, which provides strength and resilience in the face of workplace pressures.

Beyond our individual roles, we can contribute to a more positive and faith-filled work environment by modeling ethical behavior, demonstrating compassion, and fostering supportive relationships. Seeking opportunities to mentor younger colleagues, offering encouragement to those struggling, and creating a culture of mutual respect and collaboration can transform the workplace into a more uplifting and spiritually nourishing environment. This transforms the workplace from a mere place of employment to a context for serving others and demonstrating Christ-like character. By proactively creating a positive atmosphere, we can extend God's influence into the hearts and minds of our colleagues.

In conclusion, integrating faith into our career and work life is not about separating our spiritual and professional selves, but about harmonizing them. It's about seeing our work not as a mere job, but as a calling, a vocation, and an opportunity to serve God and others. By applying biblical principles of diligence, integrity, and service, we can find fulfillment, purpose, and spiritual growth in our professional endeavors. It requires intentionality, prayer, and a commitment to living out our faith in every aspect of our lives, transforming our workplaces into environments that honor God and bless those around us. This holistic approach to work empowers us to live out our faith in a profound and transformative way, enriching both our professional lives and our spiritual journeys. The journey may be challenging at times, but the rewards – both material and spiritual – are immeasurable.

CHAPTER 18

BUILDING STRONG FAMILY RELATIONSHIPS

Building strong family relationships, the bedrock of a thriving society, requires a conscious effort and a commitment to biblical principles. The scriptures offer a wealth of wisdom regarding marriage, parenting, and sibling relationships, providing a framework for creating a loving, supportive, and God-honoring family unit. These principles, when consistently applied, can transform familial interactions, fostering deeper bonds and enriching the lives of every member.

The foundation of a strong family rests upon the marriage relationship. Ephesians 5:22-33 provides a powerful model for husbands and wives: "Wives, submit to your husbands as to the Lord. For the husband is the head of the wife as Christ is the head of the church, his body, of which he is the Savior. Now as the church submits to Christ, so also wives should submit to their husbands in everything. Husbands, love your wives, just as Christ loved the church and gave himself up for her..." This passage doesn't advocate for subservience, but rather for mutual respect, love, and selfless service within the marriage. The husband is called to sacrificially love his wife, mirroring Christ's love for the church, while the wife is called to submit to her husband's leadership, recognizing his role as the head of the family. This submission is not about power dynamics, but about a complementary partnership where each spouse cherishes the other and seeks their mutual well-being. Open communication, active listening, and a willingness to compromise are essential ingredients for cultivating a healthy and loving marriage. Regular date nights, shared activities, and intentional time spent together nurture intimacy and strengthen the bond between husband and wife. Moreover, it's crucial to prioritize prayer and Bible study together, grounding the relationship in a shared faith and seeking God's guidance in navigating life's challenges.

Parenting, another crucial aspect of family life, requires wisdom, patience, and unwavering love. Deuteronomy 6:4-9 emphasizes the importance of instilling faith in children from a young age: "Hear, O Israel: The Lord our God, the Lord is one. Love the Lord your God with all your heart and with all your soul and with all your strength. These commandments that I give you today are to be on your hearts. Impress them on your children. Talk about them when you sit at home and when you walk along the road, when you lie down, and when you get up. Tie them as symbols on your hands and bind them on your foreheads. Write them on the doorframes of your houses and on your gates." This passage highlights the responsibility of parents to actively teach their children about God's love and His commandments, not merely through words, but through consistent example and daily interaction. Discipline, when necessary, should be administered with love and understanding, aiming to correct behavior and guide children towards maturity and responsibility. It's crucial to foster open communication, creating a safe space where children feel comfortable sharing their thoughts and feelings without fear of judgment. Providing ample opportunities for children to explore their talents and passions helps build their self-esteem and confidence. Spending quality time with children, engaging in shared activities, and celebrating their achievements strengthens family bonds and fosters a sense of belonging. The goal is to raise children who are not only well-adjusted and responsible individuals, but also deeply rooted in their faith and committed to living a life that honors God.

Sibling relationships often play a significant role in shaping a child's personality and social skills. While sibling rivalry is common, it's crucial to teach children the importance of love, respect, and forgiveness. Establishing clear boundaries and expectations can minimize conflict and foster a sense of fairness. Encouraging cooperation and collaboration through shared activities can strengthen sibling bonds. Parents can mediate disputes fairly, teaching children to resolve conflicts peacefully and empathetically. Furthermore, fostering an environment of mutual support and encouragement can help siblings navigate the challenges of growing up together. Celebrating each other's achievements and offering words of comfort and encouragement during difficult times contribute to a healthy sibling dynamic. Parental guidance and intervention are often needed to help children understand and appreciate their siblings, learning to value their unique qualities and contributions to the family.

Prioritizing family time is crucial for building strong relationships. Regular family meals, shared activities, and dedicated time for conversation and connection create lasting memories and strengthen family bonds. These moments are not merely opportunities for relaxation and fun, but chances to nurture intimacy, build trust, and address any challenges or conflicts. Establishing routines and traditions strengthens family identity and unity. These traditions, whether it's a weekly family game night or an annual vacation, create shared experiences that enrich family life and build lasting memories. Creating a loving home environment is also essential. This involves fostering an atmosphere of warmth, acceptance, and mutual respect. A home where children feel safe, loved, and valued is a foundation for emotional well-being and healthy development. This atmosphere should be one that reflects Christian values, promoting love, forgiveness, and compassion. It's a sanctuary where family members can find comfort and support, knowing that they are cherished and unconditionally loved.

Faith plays a vital role in strengthening family relationships. Regular family prayer, Bible study, and church attendance provide a shared spiritual foundation and reinforce the importance of faith in daily life. This commitment to spiritual growth not only strengthens individual faith but also unites the family in a common purpose and values. Shared prayer provides an opportunity to express gratitude, seek guidance, and strengthen spiritual bonds. The family that prays together stays together, finding solace and strength in their shared faith. Moreover, faith teaches vital lessons such as forgiveness, grace, and unconditional love, which are crucial for navigating conflicts and strengthening family ties. It provides a framework for understanding life's challenges and finding hope and resilience in the face of adversity. The principles of love, compassion, and forgiveness, central to Christian teachings, are essential for cultivating healthy and fulfilling family relationships.

Building strong family relationships is an ongoing process that requires consistent effort, commitment, and a willingness to apply biblical principles. It's a journey of growth and learning, requiring patience, understanding, and a spirit of forgiveness. While challenges are inevitable, the rewards of a strong, loving family far outweigh the difficulties. The family, grounded in faith and love, becomes a haven, a place of refuge, and a source of strength and support for each member. It's a testament to God's love and a powerful reflection of His grace. The journey to build a strong family is a lifelong commitment, but one that is richly rewarding and eternally significant. The love, support, and shared experiences within a thriving family unit leave an indelible mark, shaping individuals and enriching lives for generations to come. The investment in building a strong family is an investment in building a stronger future, a future shaped by faith, love, and a commitment to biblical principles.

CHAPTER 19

OVERCOMING TEMPTATION AND MAINTAINING INTEGRITY

The journey towards success, as illuminated by biblical principles, isn't solely about achieving worldly ambitions. It's equally, if not more so, about cultivating a strong moral compass, an unwavering integrity that withstands the storms of temptation and adversity. This involves actively engaging in strategies that bolster self-control, foster resilience, and nurture a deep-seated commitment to righteousness. The path is paved with challenges, but with faith as our guide and God's grace as our strength, we can navigate these trials and emerge victorious.

One of the most effective tools in overcoming temptation is prayer. Prayer is not merely a ritual; it's a lifeline to the divine, a channel through which we seek strength, guidance, and solace. In moments of weakness, when temptation's grip tightens, turning to God in earnest prayer becomes paramount. The Bible consistently underscores the power of prayer: Philippians 4:6-7 assures us, "Do not be anxious about anything, but in every situation, by prayer and petition, with thanksgiving, present your requests to God. And the peace of God, which transcends all understanding, will guard your hearts and your minds in Christ Jesus." This passage doesn't suggest a passive reliance on prayer, but rather an active engagement with God, a consistent pouring out of our hearts and anxieties before Him. Through prayer, we invite God's intervention, seeking His wisdom to discern right from wrong and His strength to resist temptation's allure. Beyond individual prayer, engaging in corporate prayer with fellow believers can significantly enhance our resilience. Sharing our struggles and praying together creates a supportive community where we can find encouragement, accountability, and mutual support. The power of collective prayer is undeniable; James 5:16 states, "Therefore confess your sins to each other and pray for each other so that you may be healed. The prayer of a righteous person is powerful and effective." This verse highlights the transformative power of confession and intercessory prayer, emphasizing the healing and strengthening effect of communal support. Joining a faith community, whether it be a church, small group, or prayer fellowship, can provide the necessary framework for such mutual support.

Developing self-control is another critical element in maintaining integrity. This isn't about suppressing our desires or denying our emotions, but about exercising discipline and making conscious choices aligned with God's will. Proverbs 25:28 offers profound insight: "Like a city whose walls are broken down is a person who lacks self-control." This verse uses a powerful image to illustrate the vulnerability of someone lacking self-discipline. Just as a city with breached walls is susceptible to attack, so too is an individual without self-control vulnerable to temptation's destructive forces. Cultivating self-control requires deliberate practice and commitment. It involves setting realistic goals, prioritizing our time effectively, and avoiding situations that could lead to temptation. The Bible teaches us the importance of self-discipline in numerous contexts, from personal habits to financial management, emphasizing the connection between self-control and a successful, God-honoring life.

Building resilience is crucial in navigating the inevitable challenges that life throws our way. Resilience isn't about avoiding hardship, but about bouncing back from adversity, learning from setbacks, and emerging stronger. The story of Joseph in the Old Testament is a testament to the power of resilience. Despite facing betrayal, imprisonment, and false accusations, Joseph remained faithful to God and ultimately rose to a position of great influence. His story exemplifies the importance of maintaining hope, faith, and perseverance in the face of adversity. Building resilience involves cultivating a positive mindset, focusing on our strengths, and seeking support from others. It requires acknowledging our weaknesses, learning from our mistakes, and consistently striving for growth and improvement. This process of learning and growing from our experiences is vital in building resilience and maintaining our integrity in the face of challenges.

Peer pressure, a pervasive force in our society, can significantly challenge our integrity. The desire to fit in, to be accepted, can lead us to compromise our values and make choices that we later regret. The Bible warns against the dangers of following the crowd, urging us to follow God's path, irrespective of societal pressures. Proverbs 1:10-15 warns, "My son, if sinful men entice you, do not give in to them. If they say, "Come along with us; let's lie in wait for someone; let's ambush him and kill him; let's swallow him alive, like the grave, and take him down to Sheol; we will get all sorts of valuable things and fill our houses with plunder"; my son, do not go along with them, do not set foot on their paths." This passage powerfully portrays the devastating consequences of succumbing to peer pressure, highlighting the importance of maintaining our integrity and choosing our companions wisely. Resisting peer pressure often requires courage and conviction, a willingness to stand apart from the crowd and remain true to our convictions.

Accountability plays a vital role in maintaining integrity. Sharing our struggles and goals with trusted individuals can create a system of checks and balances, helping us stay on track and resist temptation. Having someone to hold us accountable provides encouragement and support, offering a sense of responsibility and preventing isolation.

This accountability could be a trusted friend, family member, mentor, or spiritual advisor. The act of confessing our weaknesses and seeking advice from others can be a powerful tool in overcoming temptations and maintaining integrity. This aligns with the biblical concept of community, where believers encourage and support one another in their spiritual journey. The biblical examples of individuals who resisted temptation and maintained their integrity provide powerful inspiration and guidance. Consider Joseph's steadfastness in the face of Potiphar's wife's advances (Genesis 39), Daniel's unwavering commitment to his faith even when facing persecution (Daniel 1-6), and Job's perseverance through unimaginable suffering (Job). These stories demonstrate that maintaining integrity is not always easy, but it is always possible through faith, prayer, and reliance on God's strength. Their struggles and triumphs serve as timeless examples of the resilience of the human spirit when guided by a deep faith.

Ultimately, overcoming temptations and maintaining integrity is a lifelong journey, not a destination. It requires consistent effort, self-awareness, and a reliance on God's grace. By integrating these practical strategies into our daily lives—prayer, self-control, resilience building, resisting peer pressure, and embracing accountability—we can fortify our moral compass and build a life that honors God and reflects His glory. The path may be challenging, but the rewards—a life of integrity, peace, and fulfillment—are immeasurable.

This journey is not a solitary endeavor; it's a shared experience, supported by the community of faith and empowered by the transformative grace of God.

CHAPTER 20

DEVELOPIING A GROWTH MIND SET

The previous section emphasized the importance of integrity, a cornerstone of a life guided by biblical principles. Building upon this foundation, we now turn to another crucial element for a successful and fulfilling life: cultivating a growth mindset. This is not merely a self-help concept; it's a deeply spiritual discipline rooted in the very nature of our relationship with God, a relationship characterized by continuous learning, growth, and transformation. The Bible, far from portraying a static image of human potential, reveals a God who constantly challenges, refines, and empowers us to become more than we initially are.

A growth mindset, in its essence, is the belief that our abilities and intelligence are not fixed traits, but rather malleable qualities that can be developed through dedication, hard work, and perseverance. This contrasts with a fixed mindset, which assumes that our capabilities are predetermined and immutable. Someone with a fixed mindset might shy away from challenges, fearing failure as a reflection of their inherent limitations. In contrast, a person with a growth mindset embraces challenges as opportunities for learning and growth, viewing setbacks not as definitive defeats but as valuable stepping stones on the path to improvement.

The biblical narrative is replete with examples of individuals who embodied this growth mindset. Consider the apostle Paul, once a fierce persecutor of Christians, who underwent a radical transformation after encountering the risen Christ on the road to Damascus (Acts 9). His subsequent life demonstrates a remarkable capacity for growth, learning, and adaptation. He embraced his past mistakes not as defining labels, but as experiences that shaped his ministry and fueled his relentless dedication to spreading the Gospel. He constantly sought to deepen his understanding of God's word, his letters showcasing a profound intellectual curiosity and a willingness to grapple with complex theological issues. His personal journey, marked by both successes and failures, epitomizes the dynamic nature of spiritual growth and underscores the power of embracing a growth mindset.

Another powerful example is found in the life of King David. Despite his profound flaws—adultery, murder, and other significant failings—David remained a man deeply loved by God. Throughout his life, he experienced periods of both immense success and devastating hardship. His psalms, expressions of his intimate relationship with God, vividly portray his emotional struggles, his repentance, and his relentless pursuit of God's favor. His journey reveals a willingness to confront his own weaknesses, to learn from his mistakes, and to persevere in his faith despite adversity. This constant striving towards spiritual growth is a testament to the transformative power of a growth mindset nurtured by faith.

The prophet Moses, initially reluctant to lead the Israelites out of Egypt, ultimately became one of the most influential figures in biblical history (Exodus 3-4). His initial hesitation, his perceived inadequacy, and his subsequent transformative journey highlight the power of God's grace and the potential for profound growth even in the face of self-doubt. Moses's transformation underscores the fact that our limitations are not insurmountable obstacles; they are challenges that, with

God's help, can be overcome through diligent effort and a commitment to continuous learning. His story serves as a powerful testament to the potential for growth within each of us.

How, then, can we cultivate this essential growth mindset? The answer lies in actively embracing several key principles:

Embrace Challenges:

Instead of avoiding challenges that lie outside our comfort zones, we should actively seek them out. This is not about recklessly jumping into every difficulty, but about intentionally stepping beyond our perceived limitations, trusting in God's strength to empower us to overcome obstacles. This aligns with the biblical principle of stretching our faith, knowing that God is faithful to see us through whatever challenges we may face. Proverbs 3:5-6 encourages us to trust in the Lord with all our hearts and not lean on our own understanding. This trust forms the foundation for embracing challenges with courage and faith.

Persevere Through Setbacks:

Failure is not the opposite of success; it's a crucial component of it. Setbacks are inevitable, but they are not insurmountable. They offer invaluable opportunities for learning and growth. Instead of succumbing to discouragement, we should view setbacks as learning experiences, analyzing what went wrong, adjusting our approach, and persevering towards our goals. The biblical account of Joseph, enduring years of hardship before ultimately achieving his God-given purpose, exemplifies the power of perseverance. His resilience, his unwavering faith, and his ability to learn from his experiences demonstrate the importance of viewing setbacks as temporary obstacles rather than permanent defeats.

Learn from Feedback:

Constructive criticism, while sometimes painful, can be an invaluable tool for growth. We should actively seek feedback from trusted individuals –mentors, friends, or family – and use it to identify areas for improvement. The Bible encourages us to seek wise counsel (Proverbs 15:22). This involves a willingness to be vulnerable, to acknowledge our weaknesses, and to accept constructive criticism as a gift. By humbly embracing feedback, we create opportunities for personal growth and transformation.

Find Inspiration in Others' Successes:

Instead of viewing others' achievements with envy or resentment, we should seek to learn from their successes and draw inspiration from their journeys. This involves a spirit of humility, recognizing that we can learn from others' experiences and that collaboration and encouragement can enhance our personal growth. This aligns with the biblical principle of community, where believers encourage and support each other in their spiritual journeys.

Focus on the Process, Not Just the Outcome:

Often, our focus is solely on achieving the end goal. However, the process itself is vital for growth and learning. By appreciating the journey, focusing on consistent effort and improvement, we foster a growth mindset that values the continuous pursuit of excellence. The biblical concept of stewardship emphasizes the importance of faithful diligence in our work, regardless of the immediate outcome.

Embrace Lifelong Learning:

Spiritual growth, much like personal growth, is a lifelong journey. We must continually seek to expand our knowledge, our skills, and our understanding. This involves a commitment to continuous learning, a willingness to embrace new challenges, and a recognition that growth is a dynamic process. This commitment to lifelong learning aligns with the biblical principle of wisdom, recognizing that true wisdom comes from the fear of the Lord (Proverbs 9:10).

By integrating these principles into our lives, we can cultivate a growth mindset rooted in faith and empowered by God's grace. This mindset will not only enhance our personal achievements but also deepen our spiritual journey, enabling us to become more Christ-like, more compassionate, and more impactful in the world around us. The path towards success, defined not merely by worldly metrics but by spiritual growth and positive impact, is paved with challenges, but with a growth mindset fueled by faith, we can navigate these trials and emerge stronger, more resilient, and closer to our divine potential. Our journey is not merely a linear progression; it's a continuous cycle of learning, growth, and transformation, constantly shaped by God's grace and our commitment to embracing a growth mindset. This journey, a testament to God's transformative power, empowers us to become more than we ever thought possible, leaving a lasting legacy that reflects His love and glory.

CHAPTER 21

THE POWER OF PRAYER AND MEDITATION

Building upon the foundation of a growth mindset, we now explore the transformative power of prayer and meditation. These aren't merely religious rituals; they are vital spiritual disciplines that profoundly impact our connection with God and contribute significantly to a successful and fulfilling life, as defined by both worldly achievements and spiritual growth. Prayer and meditation are the cornerstones of a vibrant relationship with the divine, fostering inner peace, clarity, and a deeper understanding of God's will for our lives. They are not passive activities; rather, they are active engagements that shape our perspectives, strengthen our faith, and empower us to overcome challenges with grace and resilience.

Prayer, in its simplest form, is communication with God. It's a conversation, a dialogue, a pouring out of our hearts to the divine. It encompasses adoration, confession, thanksgiving, and supplication – the full spectrum of human emotion and experience. It is not confined to formal settings or prescribed phrases; it can be a spontaneous cry of the heart, a whispered petition, or a carefully composed expression of faith. The Bible is rich with examples of diverse forms of prayer: the passionate pleas of David in the Psalms, the humble confessions of Daniel, the fervent intercessions of Moses.

These diverse examples reveal that prayer is not a rigid formula, but a dynamic expression of our relationship with God. Consider the numerous forms prayer can take:

Adoration:

This involves expressing our love, reverence, and awe for God. It's acknowledging His majesty, His power, His love, and His sovereignty. It's a humbling experience that reminds us of our place in the grand scheme of things. This type of prayer centers us on God's greatness and allows us to draw strength and inspiration from His infinite power and unwavering love.

Confession:

Honest confession is a critical aspect of a healthy spiritual life. It involves acknowledging our sins, our shortcomings, and our failures before God. It's not merely an act of admitting guilt; it's an act of repentance, a turning away from sin, and a commitment to living a life that honors God. The Bible assures us that God is faithful and just and will forgive us our sins and purify us from all unrighteousness (1 John 1:9). This act of confession clears our spiritual path, allowing for renewed communion with God.

Thanksgiving:

Expressing gratitude to God for His blessings, both big and small, is a powerful way to cultivate a heart of appreciation. It involves recognizing God's hand in our lives, acknowledging His provision, His protection, and His guidance. Thanksgiving shifts our focus from our needs to God's goodness, fostering a spirit of contentment and joy. In Philippians 4:6, Paul encourages us to "be anxious for nothing, but in everything by prayer and supplication, with thanksgiving, let your requests be made known to God."

Practicing gratitude through prayer deepens our appreciation for God's constant care.

Supplication:

This involves petitioning God for our needs and the needs of others. It's a vulnerable act, an acknowledgment of our dependence on God. It's important to remember that supplication doesn't mean demanding from God; it means humbly seeking His guidance, His wisdom, and His provision. James 1:5 reminds us that if we lack wisdom, we should ask God, who gives generously and without reproach. This act reinforces our trust in God's providence and his ability to answer our prayers according to His perfect will.

The benefits of regular prayer are numerous and profound. It fosters a deeper connection with God, strengthens our faith, reduces stress and anxiety, enhances clarity of thought, and provides guidance in decision-making. It allows us to communicate directly with the source of all wisdom, power, and love. Regular prayer builds resilience and fosters a sense of peace amidst life's storms. It empowers us to face challenges with courage, faith, and hope.

Meditation, closely related to prayer, is a practice of focused attention and contemplation. It involves quieting the mind, silencing the noise of the world, and focusing on God's presence. It's a practice of centering oneself in God's love and allowing His peace to permeate our being. Just as prayer is active communication, meditation is receptive communion. It's about creating space for God to speak to our hearts, to guide our thoughts, and to reveal His will. It's a pathway to inner stillness, a sanctuary where we can reconnect with our spiritual core.

Different forms of meditation can be employed, including:

Centering Prayer:

This involves selecting a sacred word or phrase and repeating it silently throughout the meditation. The purpose is not to analyze the word or its meaning, but to use it as a focal point to center the mind and quiet the internal dialogue.

Lectio Divina:

This method involves slowly reading and reflecting on a passage of Scripture. It's a contemplative practice that allows the word of God to penetrate our hearts and minds. It involves reading, meditating, praying, and contemplating the selected scripture.

Mindfulness Meditation:

This involves focusing on the present moment, observing our thoughts and feelings without judgment. The goal is not to eliminate thoughts, but to become aware of them without getting carried away by them. This practice enhances self-awareness and allows us to cultivate a sense of inner calm.

Nature Meditation:

This involves spending time in nature, observing the beauty and wonder of the natural world. It's a way to connect with God's creation and to experience His presence in a tangible way. This fosters a deep appreciation for God's handiwork and reminds us of his enduring love.

The benefits of regular meditation are equally profound. It reduces stress, improves focus and concentration, enhances self-awareness, promotes emotional regulation, and fosters inner peace. It's a powerful tool for stress reduction and emotional well-being, allowing us to cultivate inner calm and navigate life's challenges with greater equanimity. Regular meditation strengthens our capacity for empathy, compassion, and understanding, qualities crucial for building meaningful relationships and contributing positively to the world.

Incorporating prayer and meditation into our daily routines requires intentionality and discipline. It's not about rigidly adhering to a schedule; it's about creating space for these practices in our lives, recognizing their value, and prioritizing them. Setting aside a specific time each day, even if it's just for a few minutes, can be helpful. Finding a quiet place where we can be free from distractions is important. However, even brief moments of prayer and meditation throughout the day can be powerful, transforming mundane tasks into opportunities for spiritual connection.

The key is consistency. Just as physical exercise strengthens our bodies, spiritual disciplines like prayer and meditation strengthen our spirits. Regular practice cultivates a deeper connection with God, enhancing our resilience, increasing our wisdom, and enriching our lives in immeasurable ways. It is a journey, not a destination, requiring perseverance and commitment. The more we engage in these practices, the more deeply we'll experience their transformative power. The benefits extend beyond personal spiritual growth; they enhance our relationships, our work, and our ability to contribute positively to the world around us, aligning our lives with God's purpose and enabling us to experience a truly successful and fulfilling life, guided by His grace and wisdom. Prayer and meditation are not optional extras on the journey to success; they are essential provisions, equipping us with the spiritual strength, clarity, and peace needed to navigate the challenges and celebrate the triumphs along the way. Through consistent practice, we become more attuned to God's voice, more empowered to face adversity, and more capable of living lives that reflect His love and grace, leaving

Dr. Lucious Cooper, Jr.

a positive legacy that extends far beyond our own lifetimes.

CHAPTER 22

BIBLE STUDY AND SPIRITUAL GROWTH

Building on the foundation of prayer and meditation, we now delve into another crucial spiritual discipline: consistent Bible study. Just as physical exercise strengthens the body, regular engagement with God's Word strengthens the spirit, providing guidance, wisdom, and the strength needed to navigate life's complexities and achieve success—a success defined not solely by worldly metrics, but by a life lived in accordance with God's purpose. The Bible isn't merely a historical document; it's a living, breathing word, a powerful tool for personal transformation and spiritual growth that directly contributes to a fulfilling and successful life.

Engaging with Scripture isn't about passively reading words on a page; it's an active process of listening to God's voice, seeking His wisdom, and allowing His truth to transform our hearts and minds. It's a journey of discovery, a dialogue with the divine that unveils profound truths and practical guidance for every aspect of life. The benefits extend far beyond theoretical understanding; they translate into tangible changes in our character, our relationships, and our approach to life's challenges.

Several approaches can enhance your Bible study experience, leading to deeper understanding and application:

Inductive Bible Study:

This method emphasizes observation, interpretation, and application. Begin by carefully reading a passage, noting key words, phrases, and themes. Ask questions: Who are the main characters? What is the setting? What events unfold? What are the key teachings or principles? Then, compare your observations with commentaries and other biblical resources to gain a broader understanding of the text's historical and cultural context. Finally, consider how the passage applies to your life today. How can you apply use these principles to your daily life, your relationships, and your work? Inductive Bible study encourages active engagement with the text, fostering a deeper, more personalized understanding of God's word. Consider using journaling to record your observations, insights, and applications.

Topical Bible Study:

This approach involves studying a specific topic or theme throughout Scripture. For example, you might explore the theme of love, forgiveness, or faith, tracing its development through various books and passages. This method provides a holistic perspective on a particular aspect of God's character or His teachings. Use concordances and cross-references to identify related passages and build a comprehensive understanding of the chosen topic. Reflect on how these different perspectives on the same theme enrich your comprehension and application of biblical principles.

Chronological Bible Study:

Studying the Bible chronologically can provide a richer understanding of the unfolding narrative of God's plan for humanity. This approach offers a comprehensive historical perspective, allowing you to see the connection between different events, characters, and books. Numerous chronological Bible reading plans are available, guiding you through the Scripture in its historical sequence. Reflecting on the progression of God's story allows for a deeper appreciation of His faithfulness and His unwavering plan for salvation.

Devotional Bible Study:

This involves focusing on a smaller portion of Scripture, typically a single chapter or a few verses, for daily meditation and reflection. Use a devotional guide or create your own framework for prayerful consideration. Focus on specific verses or themes that resonate with you, and allow God's word to speak directly to your heart and circumstances. This consistent daily engagement fosters a deeper, more personal relationship with God.

Comparative Bible Study:

By comparing parallel passages or different accounts of the same event, you gain a richer appreciation of the nuances and complexities of the biblical narrative. Examine the Gospels, for instance, observing the different perspectives and emphases on the same events in the life of Jesus. This allows for a multifaceted understanding of biblical truths, enriching your comprehension of God's word. No matter which approach you choose, remember that the goal is not simply to accumulate knowledge but to transform your life. Consistent Bible study must be coupled with reflection and application. Ask yourself: What does this passage reveal about God's character? What does it teach me about myself? How can I apply these principles to my daily life? Journaling your thoughts, insights, and applications is a crucial element of this process. It facilitates reflection, reinforces learning, and helps you identify specific areas where God's guidance is needed.

Incorporating regular Bible study into your daily routine demands intentionality and discipline. Setting aside a specific time, even if it's just for 15-20 minutes each day, can make a profound difference. Creating a dedicated space free from distractions fosters a focused and prayerful environment. Experiment with different times of the day to find what best suits your schedule and energy levels. Remember, consistency is key; even brief daily engagement is more effective than sporadic, lengthy sessions.

Consider these practical strategies for incorporating Bible study into your daily life:

Utilize Bible apps:

Many helpful apps provide various translations, commentaries, and study tools, making Bible study convenient and accessible. Explore features like daily devotions, verse-of-the-day notifications, and search capabilities.

Join a Bible study group:

Engaging with others in a group setting fosters accountability, provides opportunities for discussion and deeper insight, and creates a supportive community for spiritual growth.

Listen to audio Bibles:

Utilize audio Bibles during commutes or other activities, allowing you to absorb God's word even while multitasking.

Use a Bible study journal:

Keep a dedicated journal to record your observations, reflections, and applications, creating a tangible record of your spiritual journey.

Pray before and after studying:

Prayerful preparation and reflective post-study prayer enhance your engagement with God's word and increase the likelihood of applying its teachings to your life.

The transformative power of consistent Bible study is undeniable. It fosters a deeper understanding of God's character, His promises, and His plan for your life. It strengthens your faith, providing guidance and resilience in the face of challenges. It equips you with wisdom, enabling you to make sound judgments and navigate life's complexities with greater clarity. It nurtures your spiritual growth, transforming your character and shaping your values. It deepens your relationship with God, fostering a sense of peace, joy, and fulfillment that extends beyond worldly achievements. It empowers you to live a purposeful life, contributing positively to the world and leaving a legacy that honors God.

Bible study is not merely an addition to a successful life; it is the foundational element upon which a truly successful and fulfilling life, blessed by God, is built. It is the spiritual nourishment that fuels your journey, providing the strength, guidance, and wisdom necessary to overcome obstacles and celebrate triumphs, all while striving to live a life that reflects God's love and grace. Embrace this vital spiritual discipline, and experience the profound transformation it brings to your life, both spiritually and practically, empowering you to achieve true and lasting success.

CHAPTER 23

FASTING AND SPIRITUAL RENEWAL

Building upon the foundational spiritual disciplines of prayer, meditation, and consistent Bible study, we now turn our attention to fasting—a powerful practice with deep biblical roots that can profoundly enhance our spiritual lives and draw us closer to God. Fasting, often misunderstood as mere self-denial, is a deliberate act of setting aside our physical needs to prioritize our spiritual connection with the Divine. It's a potent tool for spiritual renewal, introspection, and a deepening of our relationship with God.

Throughout Scripture, fasting is presented not as a legalistic requirement, but as a voluntary act undertaken for various purposes: seeking God's guidance, humbling oneself before Him, expressing repentance, demonstrating devotion, and preparing for significant spiritual events. From Moses' forty-day fast on Mount Sinai (Exodus 34:28) to Elijah's forty-day fast in the wilderness (1 Kings 19:8) to Jesus' forty-day fast before beginning His ministry (Matthew 4:1-2), fasting has been a consistent element in the lives of significant biblical figures. These examples highlight the spiritual power and significance associated with this discipline.

The types of fasting vary, each with its own purpose and intensity. A complete fast, abstaining from all food and drink, demands careful consideration and may not be appropriate for everyone. Before embarking on such a fast, it's essential to consult with your physician, especially if you have underlying health conditions. Partial fasting, such as abstaining from specific foods or meals, offers a less rigorous approach suitable for individuals who are new to fasting or have health concerns. Daniel, for instance, chose a specific diet during his fast (Daniel 1:8-16), demonstrating that the essence of fasting lies in prioritizing spiritual discipline over physical indulgence. The goal is not self-punishment, but rather self-mastery and a redirection of focus towards God.

Intermittent fasting, a popular approach in modern times, involves cycling between periods of eating and voluntary fasting on a regular schedule. This method can be easily adapted to fit different lifestyles and health conditions. There are various schedules, such as the 16/8 method (fasting for 16 hours and eating within an 8-hour window), or other variations which can be personalized. Regardless of the method chosen, the principle remains consistent: a conscious choice to prioritize spiritual engagement over physical gratification.

Beyond the physical aspects, fasting holds profound spiritual benefits. It cultivates humility, reminding us of our dependence on God for sustenance and strength. The act of willingly foregoing physical desires creates space for spiritual focus, allowing us to connect with God more deeply through prayer and meditation. Fasting can increase our sensitivity to the Holy Spirit, enhancing our ability to hear God's voice and discern His will. It allows us to break free from distractions and immerse ourselves in God's presence. In the quietness and stillness of fasting, we become more aware of our spiritual needs and vulnerabilities. It's a time for introspection, allowing us to examine our hearts, repent of sin, and align ourselves with God's will.

Moreover, fasting is a potent catalyst for spiritual renewal. It breaks the cycle of habitual patterns and provides an opportunity to reset our priorities. When we deny ourselves physical satisfaction, we cultivate a greater capacity for spiritual discipline and self-control in other areas of life. This enhanced self-discipline translates into greater effectiveness in all aspects of our lives, including our work, relationships, and service to others. The self-mastery gained through fasting enables us to resist temptations and overcome obstacles with greater resilience. This inner strength, born from spiritual discipline, becomes a powerful asset in achieving both spiritual and worldly goals.

Fasting also fosters a deeper appreciation for God's provision and blessings. Through this act of self-denial, we experience a renewed sense of gratitude for the abundance in our lives. It reminds us that our sustenance, physical and spiritual, originates from God and fosters a greater dependence on Him. This renewed sense of gratitude translates into a deeper love and devotion towards God.

However, it is crucial to approach fasting with wisdom and discernment. Fasting should never be undertaken as a form of self-punishment or a means to manipulate God. Instead, it should be a humble act of seeking a closer relationship with Him. It is equally important to maintain a balanced approach to fasting, ensuring that it doesn't negatively impact one's physical health or well-being. Consulting with spiritual leaders and medical professionals before embarking on a fast is a vital step, particularly for extended fasts. They can provide guidance and support, helping ensure a safe and spiritually enriching experience.

The duration and intensity of fasting should be tailored to individual circumstances and capabilities. Beginning with shorter, less rigorous fasts is advisable, gradually increasing the duration and intensity as one gains experience and confidence. Moreover, the overall physical and mental wellbeing of the individual should be carefully monitored during the fast. Sufficient rest, hydration, and gentle exercise are essential. Excessive physical exertion or neglecting hydration should be strictly avoided.

The experience of fasting is not always easy. It is common to encounter feelings of hunger, fatigue, or irritability. These are to be expected and, in a way, are part of the process of self-mastery and spiritual growth. The crucial aspect is to maintain a focus on the spiritual purpose of the fast. Turning to prayer and meditation during these times will strengthen one's commitment and provide solace. Remembering the goal – to connect with God more deeply – helps to manage the challenges of the fast and maintain a spiritual perspective.

Furthermore, fasting should be complemented by other spiritual disciplines, such as prayer, meditation, and Bible study. These practices provide additional opportunities for spiritual growth and deepen the impact of the fast. They act as supportive elements, nourishing the soul and fortifying the spirit during the fast. By integrating fasting with other spiritual disciplines, we create a comprehensive program for spiritual renewal and growth.

Finally, it is important to emphasize that fasting is not a magic formula for achieving success. It is a spiritual discipline that, when undertaken with the right intention and approach, can enhance our relationship with God and foster spiritual growth. Success, as defined in this book, is a holistic concept that encompasses spiritual, emotional, and material well-being. Fasting, therefore, acts as a tool to support and enhance our spiritual journey towards a truly fulfilling and successful life, blessed by God's grace. The transformative power of fasting, combined with the other disciplines we have examined, lays the groundwork for a life lived in accordance with God's purpose, leading to a life that is both successful and deeply meaningful. It is a journey of growth, humility, and unwavering faith, leading to a life of profound purpose and enduring satisfaction. Embrace this spiritual discipline, and experience the transformative power it offers, bringing you closer to God and empowering you to achieve true and lasting success, defined not by worldly measures alone, but by a life lived in accordance with God's divine plan.

Author Biography

Dr. Lucious Cooper, Jr. is a distinguished biblical scholar, motivational speaker, retired military officer, property manager, scientist, and author, whose diverse career reflects a profound commitment to excellence and service. With an academic background that spans multiple disciplines, Dr. Cooper holds a Bachelor's degree in Radiologic Technology, a Master of Arts in Organizational Management, a Master of Science in Nuclear Science and Engineering, and a PhD in Humanities. His educational journey has equipped him with a unique perspective that he brings to his work in both the spiritual and scientific realms.

Dr. Cooper dedicated 20 years of his life to military service, where he achieved the rank of Major and was instrumental in training tens of thousands of soldiers in Nuclear, Biological, and Chemical Defense. His leadership and expertise in these critical areas earned him several military awards, recognizing his dedication to the safety and preparedness of his fellow service members. His military experience not only shaped his character but also instilled in him the values of discipline, perseverance, and faith.

In addition to his military achievements, Dr. Cooper has excelled as a property manager and scientist, where his analytical skills and attention to detail have led to successful ventures in real estate and research. His ability to balance these various roles has allowed him to develop a holistic approach to life and success, which he passionately shares with others.

As a biblical scholar and motivational speaker, Dr. Cooper

seeks to inspire individuals from all walks of life. His teachings focus on the intersection of faith and success, illustrating how spiritual principles can unlock God's blessings in one's life. Through his speaking engagements and writings, including his latest work, "The Path to Success: Unlocking God's Blessings," Dr. Cooper empowers others to pursue their dreams while remaining grounded in their faith.

Dr. Lucious Cooper, Jr. continues to be a beacon of hope and inspiration, guiding others on their journeys toward success and fulfillment. His life story is a testament to the power of faith, resilience, and the unwavering pursuit of knowledge.

www.YourAuthorWebsite.com

Made in the USA
Columbia, SC
05 May 2025